ROMANS 7
The Watershed Chapter of Scripture

Vic Reasoner

2120 Culverson Ave
Evansville, IN 47714-4811

© 2025 Victor Paul Reasoner
ISBN 979-8-9937696-0-8
Library of Congress Control Number: 2025950075

TABLE of CONTENTS

The Controversy Introduced 4
The Exegesis of Romans 7:7-35 12
The Theological Positions 48
    The Patristic Interpretation 48
    The Calvinistic Interpretation 55
    The Keswick/Dispensational Interpretation 61
    The Wesleyan-Arminian Interpretation 70
    The Holiness Interpretation 86
    Recent Developments 92
Bibliography 102

Part One: The Controversy Introduced

SOLD OUT AT ROMANS 7

Published in *The Arminian Magazine* 10:1 (Spring 1991) 7-10.

The church fathers, until Augustine in the fifth century, generally interpreted Romans 7 as pre-Christian experience. According to Augustine the conflict of Romans 7 remains the highest stage of Christian experience. To this day Calvinists usually follow Augustine, interpreting Romans 7 as Christian experience. "The Arminian controversy really began upon the exegesis of this passage," according to M. B. Riddle in *Lange's Commentary*.[1]

Jacob Hermansz was a Dutch theologian of the late sixteenth century. We know him by his Latin name, Jacobus Arminius. He went to Geneva to study under John Calvin's successor, Theodore Beza. He returned to Amsterdam to pastor. He had the reputation of being a brilliant preacher, a gifted Bible exegete, and a humble and dedicated Christian. His expositional preaching drew large crowds.

He was considered the greatest scholar of his day. He was the first ever to receive the Doctor of Divinity degree from the University of Leiden. He was a later professor of theology at the university, until his death in 1609.

---

[1] *Lange's Commentary*, 5:245.

In 1589 Dirck Coornhert declared that the supralapsarian theory of Beza actually made God the author of sin. Arminius was commissioned to answer this charge. He finally concluded that Coornhert was right. No one could refute his scholarship, but preachers began to openly attack him from the pulpit. His words were twisted out of context and his enemies tried to destroy his influence. Finally, he asked for a public hearing, but he died before the synod convened. He was about 49 when he died, and his death was probably hastened by the stress he was under.

Although it was Arminius who had called for an open forum, the Synod of Dort (1618-9) only solidified the Calvinistic position. His followers, the Remonstrants, were not allowed to enter into the debate. They were either put to death, banished, or imprisoned. They were unable to hold any office in the church or state until 1625, when they were granted limited tolerance.

The writings of Arminius have been compiled in three volumes. The second longest treatise we have is his "Dissertation on the True and Genuine Sense of the Seventh Chapter of the Epistle to the Romans." It runs 258 pages.

Within one hundred years after his death, the Remonstrants had drifted toward Pegalianism. It was John Wesley who led a move back to evangelical Arminianism, even naming his magazine The Arminian.

The early Methodists held that Romans 7 was not a description of Christian experience. Wesley said, "To have spoken this of himself, or any true believer, would have been foreign to the whole scope of his discourse."[2] Wesley saw verses 7-25 as a digression by Paul. Adam Clarke stated, "The very genius of Christianity demonstrates that nothing like this

---

[2]Wesley, *Notes*, 379.

can, with any propriety, be spoken of a genuine Christian."[3] John Fletcher devoted an entire section to Romans 7 in his "Last Check to Antinomianism." He challenged the Calvinists to drop "the yoke of carnality which they try to fix upon St. Paul's neck."[4] Richard Watson summarized the seventh and eighth chapters of Romans, saying:

> The moral state of man is traced in the experience of St. Paul as an example, from his conviction for sin by the law of God revealed to him in its spirituality, to his entrance into the condition and privilege of a justified state.[5]

The Holy Spirit is only mentioned once in the entire chapter (verse 6). He is referred to some twenty times in the following chapter. Romans 7 makes no mention of the grace of God. It is a classic psychological analysis of the struggle between the conscience and the will. Every sinner knows the conflict between what he ought to do and what he wants to do. Desire usually wins out over duty.

The Greek personal pronoun *ego* is used eight times in this description. In Greek, as with many other languages, the subject is understood in the verb. Paul supplied an additional word (*ego*) for emphasis. He does not use it once in chapter 8. Chapter 7 closes with a double pronoun in verse 25, "I myself." Paul describes a man trying to be a Christian by himself.

But many people are bothered by a change in the verb

---

[3]Clarke, *Commentary*, 6:92.

[4]Fletcher, *Works*, 2:544.

[5]Watson, *Theological Institutes*, 2:249.

tense. Through verse 13, the aorist tense was used. Then Paul switched to the present tense and used it through the end of the chapter. J. I. Packer declared, "Grammatically, therefore, the natural way to read it would be as a transcript of Paul's self-knowledge at the time of writing." He argued the present tense must have a present reference and describe something distinct from the past experience of the previous verses.[6]

Calvinists are correct in observing the fact of the tense change. They are incorrect in their interpretation of what that fact signifies. In this case, a careful reading of the context will shed a great deal of light on the commentaries! This digression is introduced by the clear statement found in 6:14 and concluded by an equally clear summary in 8:2. Salvation delivers from sin.

How can the context be harmonized with the switch in verb tenses In *A Manual Grammar of the Greek New Testament*, we are told one of the special uses of the present tense is the "historical present." "The present tense is thus employed when a past event is viewed with the vividness of a present occurrence."[7] Today this literary technique is called a *flashback*. Whether or not this is accepted as the proper interpretation for Romans 7:14-25 probably depends upon your own theological presuppositions. The explanation that Paul is remembering his pre-Christian experience is allowed by Greek grammar, however.

Recently a leading Calvinistic exponent, Anthony Hoekema, Calvin Seminary professor emeritus, reversed himself and declared that he no longer believes Romans 7 describes a regenerate person. He stated:

---

[6]Packer, *Keeping in Step with the Spirit*, 264.

[7]Dana and Mantey, *Manual Grammar*, 185.

The mood of frustration and defeat that permeates this section does not comport with the mood of victory in terms of which Paul usually describes the Christian life. The person pictured is still a captive of the law of sin (7:23), whereas the believer described in 6:17-18 is no longer a slave to sin.[8]

That kind of intellectual honesty is rare. How would he have fared at the Synod of Dort? While Hoekema's comments are refreshing, it is very disheartening to read comments and hear sermons coming from the holiness movement on Romans 7. Keep in mind that these men consider themselves defenders of Wesleyan-Arminian orthodoxy. W. B. Godbey said:

> Every Christian, when converted, sets out to obey the Lord on earth like the angels in heaven, thus keeping the law in the beauty of holiness; but destined to defeat, failure, mortification despondency, culminating is desperation, like Paul in the verse when he cried out, "O wretched man that I am!"[9]

H. C. Morrison wrote:

> The Christian reader will at once recognize the undoubted truthfulness of these Scriptures for they are corroborated by the every-day experience of believing souls, who, struggling against the "old man," have often been made to cry out, "O wretched man

---

[8]Hoekema, "Response to Walvoord," 232.

[9]Godbey, *Commentary*, 5:104.

that I am, who shall deliver me from the body of this death."[10]

For Morrison, the solution to this problem is to receive the baptism with the Holy Ghost, which he equates with entire sanctification. Early Methodism taught that occurred along with justification.

Charles Ewing Brown explained what he thought Romans 7:7-25 meant:

> Assuming, then, that we have in this chapter an account of the experience of a true and even of an advanced Christian, we learn that in every Christian there is a mixture of good and evil.[11]

In *Great Holiness Classics: Holiness Teaching Today*, not only are the statements by Morrison and Brown reprinted, but Milton Agnew describes Christian experience:

> After conversion he discovers in himself a new nature that does "joyfully concur with the law of God" (Romans 7:22). But he learns to his distress that he also has an old nature, an "old self," aroused and battling for supremacy. There occurs a profoundly disturbing struggle between the two natures, the two "I's" of 7:14-25.[12]

---

[10]Morrison, *Baptism with the Holy Ghost*, 24.

[11]Brown, *The Meaning of Sanctification*, 27.

[12]Agnew, *More Than Conquerors*, cited in *Holiness Teaching Today*, 146.

William Greathouse, writing in *Beacon Bible Commentary*, admits the primary meaning of Romans 7 is the unrenewed man. Yet he claims that the passage has a secondary meaning in which it describes a carnal babe in Christ.[13] We are warned in *Biblical Hermeneutics* that "if the Scripture has more than one meaning, it has no meaning at all."[14]

Nazarene scholar Ralph Earle encouraged preachers to apply Romans 7 both before and after conversion in *Word Meanings in the New Testament*.[15] Therefore, fellow Nazarene Kenneth Grider seems to be overly optimistic when he asserts that "anyone in the Holiness movement knows that a regenerate person does not sin willfully, and yet this person depicted in Romans 7 seems to do that." He blames the "folk theology" of ministers and teachers for spreading the idea that Romans 7 depicts a saved man.[16] But as long as his denomination is reprinting *Great Holiness Classics*, which are not necessarily great classics nor Wesleyan, it is hard to pin all the blame on the uneducated.

Is it any wonder the pew is confused when the pulpit sounds an uncertain note? Is it any wonder the student is unclear when the teacher tries to ride the fence?

It does matter what we believe about Romans 7. Our interpretation of the passage is like a watershed. Whichever way we go will lead us to drastically different theological

---

[13]Greathouse, "Romans," 159-160. Greathouse takes a more Wesleyan position in his second commentary on Romans some forty years later. See *Romans 1-8*, 222-223.

[14]Terry, *Biblical Hermeneutics*, 493. Terry was quoting John Owen.

[15]Earle, *Word Meanings*, 3:135-137.

[16]Grider, *Entire Sanctification*, 141-142.

conclusions. The man described in Romans 7 was a slave to sin. It is true that he is unsanctified; he is also unsaved. We need not discount regeneration in order to make room for sanctification. For too long the holiness movement has tried to establish the need for a second work by demonstrating the failure of the first work.

Let us declare a moratorium on such illustrations as supposed Christians losing their temper and kicking the cow, biting the cow, or beating the cow. According to Galatians 5:20, outbursts of anger are a work of the flesh. Those who belong to Christ have crucified the flesh. Those who walk after the flesh will not inherit the kingdom of God. True Christians are enabled by the Spirit to control sinful desires. Entire sanctification is a completion or perfection of what God began in regeneration. If nothing changed when we got saved, then we are simply making two trips to the altar to get saved, and claiming we have the second blessing. If we accept the second blessing on the basis of logical deduction, it is possible to have made two or more trips forward and still be a slave to sin.

The holiness movement has adopted the theology of John Calvin, while claiming to be the defender of John Wesley. No wonder we profess so much and live so far short of our profession.

Part Two: The Exegesis of Romans 7:7-25

At vv 7 and 14 Paul introduces his argument with the use of the first-person plural (we), then shifts back into the first-person singular (I) to make his case. While he is likely giving his autobiography, the implications are broader than his individual case. We have all broken the law of God.

It has been Paul's pattern to first state a doctrine, then illustrate it. He illustrated justification by faith from Abraham's life in chapter 4. In chapter 5 he illustrates the work of Christ by contrasting it with Adam's works. Now he illustrates the freedom which comes with salvation by sharing from his own experience of bondage to sin prior to saving faith.

1. The law was not the problem 7:7-13

The law is a diagnostic tool which identifies, but does not cure the problem. Sutcliffe said, "The law is a reflection of the moral glory of God, shining out in all its purity. It shines into the heart, discovering the turpitude of sin, and all its enmity against the light."[17] The law acts as a curb, restraining sinful man as a mirror convicting the awakened man, and as a guide for the Christian. Ambroister wrote that the law is not

---

[17]Sutcliffe, *Commentary*, 2:456.

sin, but the yardstick of sin.[18]

Liberal sociology has advocated the overthrow of all law and prohibition because, they say, it incites violations of the law. But in opposing restraint, they are only encouraging lawlessness. Paul advocates the necessity of civil law in 13:1-6. The problem lies not with the law, but with the sinner. That is Paul's message to the antinomian. The law is good (v 16). The law merely locates the problem, which is sin. To blame God's law for causing sin is a type of denial.

Paul then gives a personal example. The law prohibited coveting. The fact that he was in violation of this law made Paul conscious of his sin and spiritual death. Binney wrote that in the unregenerate, sin may lie in a dormant, inactive state.[19] Sinners may ignorantly, or as Benson said, "in my own conceit,"[20] deem themselves blameless; but when the law is brought home to their soul, sin is revived by the law. It is as if sin springs from the dead. Summers wrote that v 9 depicted the unawakened, unconcerned sinner. The same person, now awakened, cries out in v 24 and is regenerated in chapter 8. The unawakened sinner has one judgment and one will: he chooses nothing but sin. The awakened sinner weakly chooses holiness, but his will cannot produce it. The regenerate man does both; he not only approves of holiness but he chooses holiness.[21]

---

[18]Ambrosiaster, *ACT*, 55. "Ambrosiaster" means the star of Ambrose and is the name given to the anonymous author of a standard Latin commentary produced by the end of the 4th century.

[19]Binney, *TPC*, 410.

[20]Benson, *Notes*, 5:60.

[21]Summers, *Commentary*, 82, 88. Summers also suggested that Paul describes the unawakened period in his own life in

Paul may also be describing one who has just reached the "age of accountability." Bruce suggested the occasion might have been Paul's *bar mitzvah*, when he became "a son of the law" at thirteen and recognized his responsibility to know and obey the ten commandments.[22]

All of us were once saved through the unconditional benefits of Christ's atonement; but yielding to the impulse of our sinful nature, when we consciously choose to violate the command of God, we die spiritually at that moment. Dayton wrote that everyone "'sins away' the grace of infancy and confirms himself in sin and death. In this sense all sinners are backsliders."[23] In Ephesians 2:1-5 Paul included himself among those who were spiritually dead. He was not alive at that time; his death was a loss of the life he had in his days of innocency.[24] Lloyd-Jones suggested that Paul's experience, given in vv 7-13, may correspond to his experience in Acts 9:5-9.[25]

Benson felt that the deception mentioned in v 11 was an allusion to the excuse made by Eve. He paraphrased v 11:

> Satan, the grand enemy of mankind, and author of sin, finding a law which threatened death to the transgression of it, takes occasion thence more ear-

---

Philippians 3:4-11 [p. 84].

[22]Bruce, *Commentary*, 147.

[23]Dayton, *Wesleyan Bible Commentary*, 5:49.

[24]Beet, *Commentary*, 197-198.

[25]Lloyd-Jones, *The Law*, 173-174. This connection fits well with the statement by Wesley that Paul was "in the pangs of the new birth" [*Notes*, 299].

nestly to tempt and allure us to the violation of it, that so he may more effectually subject us to condemnation and death upon that account. Thus, when God had forbidden, under the pain of death, the eating of the forbidden fruit, Satan thence took occasion to tempt our first parents to the breach of it, and so slew them, or made them subject to death.[26]

Sinful tendencies can lie dormant; but under close biblical preaching, rebellion comes alive. While the preaching of God's Word heightens the tension, the man of God dare not hold back. Some will be more upset after they come to church than they were before they started coming. The most loving act the preacher can perform is to so faithfully teach the truth that the problem is brought to the surface and the sinner is brought to point of crisis. The law functions as a poultice or compress which brings sin to a head. "It takes a carpenter's level to make clear how far from straight a board really is."[27] Therefore, the early Methodists first preached the law, then grace. The law is the standard of righteousness. Clarke declared, "The *law*, therefore is the grand instrument in the hands of a faithful minister, to alarm and awaken sinners; and he may safely show that every sinner is *under* the law, and consequently under the curse, who has not fled for refuge to the hope held out by the Gospel."[28] This method was also practiced by the Puritans, and they called it a preliminary

---

[26]Benson, *Notes*, 5:60.

[27]Mickelsen, *Wycliffe Bible Commentary*, 1203. Clarke made a similar comment [*Commentary*, 6:83].

[28]Clarke, *Commentary*, 6:86.

"law work."²⁹

Paul states in v 7 that he had not known his lust was sin except for the condemnation of his unlawful desires by the law. The word ἐπιθυμία (*epithumia*), used in vv 7-8, means strong desires, whether good of bad. This same word also appears in 1:24. In both cases the context would indicate a bad connotation. However, the word does not inherently carry a negative connotation. Nor is the meaning of the word restricted to unbridled or illicit forms of sexual desire. It is used by Paul in a positive sense in Philippians 1:23 and 1 Thessalonians 2:17; 3:2. Gagnon explained that "desire becomes a problem only when people are 'desirers of evil things,' such as idolatry and sexual immorality" (1 Cor 10:6; compare with Col 3:5).³⁰

The KJV translates *epithumia* in v 8 as *concupiscence*, which simply means covetousness or any kind of wrong desire. By reducing this illicit desire to the sex drive, Augustine perpetuated an error which he borrowed from pagan philosophy.³¹ William Greathouse wrote, "The church has found it almost impossible to rid itself of the feeling that carnality is virtually synonymous with sexual desire. The New Testament knows no such identification of human nature with sin."³² While sexual desire must be disciplined and channeled into the confines of marriage, while we are tempted through

---

²⁹Lloyd-Jones, *The Law*, 114.

³⁰Gagnon, *The Bible and Homosexual Practice*, 232.

³¹Freud also traced everything back to a basic sex drive, but the Scripture identifies the problem as the sin nature. See a discussion of this by Carter, *A Contemporary Wesleyan Theology*, 2:980.

³²Greathouse, *From the Apostles to Wesley*, 69-70. See also Dunning, *Grace, Faith and Holiness*, 389-390.

our sexual desires and that vulnerability can easily lead to sins of immorality, sexual desire, in and of itself, is not sin. Paul does not specify what he desired which was contrary to the law. James Macknight (1721-1800) wrote:

> He might complain of the existence of concupiscence in his mind, but if it was suffered to remain there uncontrolled, and if it hindered the actings of his sanctified will so effectually, that he never did that which he inclined, but always the evil which his sanctified will did not incline, is not this the clearest proof that concupiscence or evil desire was the prevailing principle in his mind, and that his sanctified will had no power to restrain its workings? Now, could the apostle give any plainer description of an unregenerate person than this?[33]

Yet Augustine regarded Romans 7 as the Christian's struggle with concupiscence, not the act of sinning. It was not until Jerome that we have any record of a theologian who attempts to use Romans 7 to justify his own personal lapses into sin. Jerome wrote:

> For we do not what we would but what we would not; the soul desires to do one thing, the flesh is compelled to do another. If any persons are called righteous in scripture . . . they are called righteous according to that righteousness mentioned in the passage I have quoted: "A just man falleth seven times and rises up again,". . . Zachariah the father of

---

[33]Macknight, *Apostolical Fathers with a Commentary and Notes*, 93.

John who is described as a righteous man sinned in disbelieving the message sent to him and was at once punished with dumbness. Even Job, who at the outset of his history is spoken of as perfect and upright and uncomplaining, is afterwards proved to be a sinner both by God's words and by his own confession. If Abraham, Isaac, and Jacob, the prophets also and the apostles were by no means free from sin and if the finest wheat had chaff mixed with it, what can be said of us of whom it is written: "What is the chaff to the wheat, saith the Lord?"[34]

Jerome, by his own admission was a man prone to sin. In a discussion with Ctesiphon which involved Romans 7, he confessed, "Yet to lay bare my own weakness, I know that I wish to do many things which I ought to do and yet cannot. For while my spirit is strong and leads me to life my flesh is weak and draws me to death."[35]

In his sermon "The Original, Nature, Properties, and Use of the Law," Wesley observed that most who read Romans assume the references to the law mean the Jewish law and that it does not apply to them. Wesley argued that Paul is referring to the moral law in this chapter. Although every believer is free from the Jewish ceremonial law, the entire Mosaic dispensation, and even the moral law as a means of procuring our justification, yet, in another sense, we are not through with the law. The moral law can never pass away, since it has always coexisted with God's nature. It is a copy of the eternal mind, a transcript of the divine nature. Although we are no

---

[34]Jerome, *Letter* to *Rusticas* (AD 406), 122:3 *NPNF* 2.6:228-229.

[35]Jerome, *Letter* to Ctesiphon (AD 415), 133:9. *NPNF* 2.6:278.

longer under the Jewish dispensation, the moral law still stands. It slays the sinner, destroying the life and strength in which he trusts, convincing him that he is spiritually dead. The law also functions as a schoolmaster, driving us to Christ (Gal 3:24). Third, the law keeps us alive and shows us how a Christian is to live. Nathaniel Burwash observed that the true liberty of God's people is not liberty from the *law*, but from *sin*.[36] From vv 7-9 Stott wrote that the law reveals sin, provokes sin, and condemns sin.[37]

Writing from a Calvinistic position, Greg Bahnsen taught that the law also had three functions: political, pedagogic, and didactic.[38] While Bahnsen broadened the first function to cover all of society and not just the individual, the second and third functions correspond exactly with Wesley.

Romans 7:7-13 illustrate the first use of the law as applied to the individual. The law detects the hidden things of darkness and drags them out into the open day. Wesley preached:

> 'Tis true, by this means (as the Apostle observes, verse 13) "sin appears to be sin." All its disguises are torn away, and it appears in its native deformity. 'Tis true likewise that "sin by the commandment becomes exceeding sinful." Being now committed against light and knowledge, being stripped even of the poor plea of ignorance, it loses its excuse as well as disguise, and becomes far more odious both to

---

[36]Burwash, *Wesley's Doctrinal Standards*, 333-334. Wesley's sermon is #34.

[37]Stott, *Romans*, 202-203.

[38]Bahnsen, *By This Standard*, 202.

God and man. Yea, and it is true that "sin worketh death by that which is good," which in itself is pure and holy. When it is dragged out to light it rages the more: when it is restrained it bursts out with greater violence. Thus the Apostle, speaking in the person of one who was convinced of sin but not yet delivered from it, "sin taking occasion by the commandment", detecting and endeavoring to restrain it, disdained the restraint, and so much the more "wrought in me all manner of concupiscence" (verse 8)—all manner of foolish and hurtful desire, which that commandment sought to restrain. Thus "when the commandment came, sin revived" (verse 9). It fretted and raged the more. But this is no stain on the commandment. Though it is abused it cannot be defiled. This only proves that "the heart" of man "is desperately wicked." But "the law" of God "is holy" still.[39]

2. Sin caused us to break the law 7:14-25

The verbs in vv 7-13 were past (aorist) tense. Although the verbs now switch to the present tense, this is not conclusive evidence that Paul is describing his current condition. Packer wrote:

> Paul's shift from the past tense to the present in verse 14 has no natural explanation save that he now

---

[39]Wesley, "The Original, Nature, Properties, and Use of the Law," Sermon #34, 3.4. While Wesley gave three uses of the law, he did not teach that we can earn salvation through keeping the law — which is legalism.

moves on from talking about his experience with God's law in his pre-Christian days to talking about his experience as it was at the time of writing. Any other view represents him as an inept communicator who, by making a needless and pointless change of tense, was asking to be misunderstood.[40]

Yet the interpretation is not that simple. Packer's solution raises more questions than it answers. Peter did say that Paul's epistles contained some things that were hard to understand (2 Peter 3:16). William Williams wrote, "But though there is a change of tense, there is no new phase of experience; only a new accentuation of the old, and we must date all experiences so described back to the dispensation of law."[41] Lloyd-Jones cautioned, "We must not be carried away by the notion that the mere change in the tense establishes the only possible interpretation of this particular section."[42]

There are two interpretive issues to be resolved. Is this account autobiographical or is Paul impersonating the common experience of every person? Grammatically, this impersonation is called *prosopopoeia*.

The more critical question is the tense shift. Ben Witherington argued that the *I* in Romans 7 is Adam. Thus, vv 7-13 are in the past, describing Adam's sin; and vv 14-25 are in the present tense describing all who are in Adam.[43]

Present tense verbs are sometimes used as a historical present. Boyce Blackwelder explained, "The Apostle Paul

---

[40]Packer, *Keep in Step with the Spirit*, 143-144, 263-270.

[41]William Williams, *Exposition*, 227.

[42]Lloyd-Jones, *The Law*, 184.

[43]Witherington, *The Problem with Evangelical Theology*, 21-37.

uses the historical present tense in his vivid description of the spiritual battle which once raged in his life."[44] Thus, Paul used the present tense to make vivid his past struggles or to depict the present struggle of the unregenerate. However, this could not be his present condition.

Blackwelder also said that v 14 "apparently depicts the state of an unregenerate person bound by fetters he cannot break." The fact that Paul used the present tense "does not necessarily mean that he is describing his condition at the time of writing." Blackwelder claimed that the use of the historical present was common in Koine Greek and that the use of γάρ (*gar*- translated *for* in the KJV and not translated in the NIV) "connotes an explanation and continuation of the thought of the previous section."[45]

Burwash observed that at v 5 Paul moved from the second to the first person plural, thus identifying himself in this common experience of the effect of the law. In v 7 he passes from the plural to the singular as the vividness of the subject in its relationship to his personal experience grows. This, however, does not make his account an exclusively personal experience. "He still describes the common experience of the effects of the law." So, in v 14, while declaring that the law is spiritual, Paul uses the present tense. His whole discourse from this point onward is an enunciation of a present reality in fallen human nature. His vivid description may well be explained by the fact that few men had a more profound revelation of fallen human nature. But it by no means follows that because we recognize his reference to his own experience

---

[44]Blackwelder, *Light from the Greek New Testament*, 67.

[45]Blackwelder, *Toward Understanding Romans*, 54-55. See also Oden, *Life in the Spirit*, 245-246.

in this general description that we should transfer his unregenerate experience under the law to his new position under grace.[46]

While Paul said in v 13 that sin was working death in him, in 6:7 he said that anyone who had died has been freed from sin. While he said in v 14 that he is carnal, having been sold under sin, in 8:2 he says he is free from the law of sin and death. While in v 15 he says, "What I hate I do," he wrote to the Thessalonians, "You are witnesses of how holy, righteous and blameless we were among you" (1 Thess 2:10). He boasts that he can do all things through Christ (Phil 4:13). While he cries out in v 24, "What a wretched man I am!," in 2 Corinthians 6:10 he declares that he is always rejoicing. Henry Williams concluded that to imagine Paul is describing his own state when he wrote this epistle is to violate all consistency.[47]

Coke declared that if by using the first person singular Paul "meant himself or any other person who had embraced the Gospel, then his argument would prove the insufficiency of the Gospel, as well as of the law." Coke then paraphrased v 14:

> For we all are agreed that the law is spiritual, requiring actions pure and rational, and quite opposite to those which our carnal affections dictate. But I, the sinner, am carnal, under the dominion of sensual appetite and the habits of sin, and for that reason condemned by the law: the fault is not in the law, but in me the sinner, as appears hence; — that which

---

[46]Burwash, *Handbook*, 133-134.

[47]Henry Williams, *Exposition*, 198.

I do, I allow not.[48]

Benson commented that man, "destitute of the regenerating grace of God, *is carnal.*" He interpreted the phrase "in the flesh" (v 5), as well as similar expressions in 8:5, 8, and 9, as representing a state of death and enmity against God, which refers solely to the unregenerate. The spiritual man is in a very different state. The Spirit of God dwells in him, giving him dominion over all fleshly lusts. His passions submit to reason and his reason is under the influence of grace. "The Scriptures, therefore, place these two characters in direct opposition the one to the other."[49]

Yet Max Lucado declared that, because Paul was writing in the present tense, "He is not describing a struggle of the past, but a struggle in the present. For all we know, Paul was engaged in spiritual combat even as he wrote this letter."[50] However, the issue is more than spiritual combat; it is spiritual bondage and defeat. Paul was not overcome by sin; he was carried along by the Holy Spirit (2 Pet 1:21). Ironically, the direct inspiration of the Spirit can produce a manuscript without error, but not an apostle without sin, according to dispensationalists.

Abrosiaster held that a free mind can repulse evil temptations by the help of the Holy Spirit. If it is no longer subject to sin, then Satan cannot appear uninvited.

A cure has been found by the providence of God, so that the salvation which man had lost by his own

---

[48]Coke, *Commentary*, 5:76.

[49]Benson, *Notes*, 5:61.

[50]Lucado, *In the Grip of Grace*, 145.

fault might be given back to him. Now that he had been born again he can believe, because his adversary, defeated by the power of Christ, would not dare to rely on the sentence of the first death, which has now been superseded in the reconciled race of Adam.[51]

Although the NIV omits *for*, verse 14 begins with the particle γάρ (*gar*) which connects this verse to what has preceded it. Arminius argued that since the same subject is under discussion, the *I* must be understood as relating to the same man, a man who was under the law, and not introducing a new subject, a man under grace.

The Scriptures do not speak of the regenerate as "carnal." They are not in the flesh (*sarx*), but in the Spirit (8:9). Those who are carnal (*sarx*) cannot please God (8:8), but the regenerate please God because they have their mind set on what the Spirit desires (8:5). Therefore, the regenerate are not carnal.[52]

Paul also states in Romans 7:14 that he was sold under sin. Benson said that this added clause demonstrates that Paul did not use the word *carnal* in the sense in which it is used in 1 Corinthians 3:1, which describes new converts who are in a state of imperfection in knowledge and holiness.[53]

Although James Macknight was Presbyterian he wrote:

> Because the apostle in this passage uses the first person, "I am sold,"&c. Augustine in the latter part of his life and most of the commentators after his

---

[51] Ambrosiaster, *ACT*, 60-61.

[52] Arminius, *Works*, 2:513.

[53] Benson, *Notes*, 5:62.

time, with many of the moderns, especially the Calvinists, contend, that in this, and in what follows, to the end of the chapter, the apostle described his own state at the time he wrote this epistle, consequently the state of every regenerated person. But most of the ancient Greek commentators, all the Arminians, and some Calvinists, hold, that though the apostle speaks in the first person, he by no means describes his own state, but the state of an unregenerated sinner awakened, by the operation of law, to a sense of his sin and misery. And this opinion they support by observing, that in his writings the apostle often personates others. See Rom. xiii.11-13. Wherefore, to determine the question, the reader must consider to which of the two characters the things written in this chapter best agree; and in particular, whether the apostle could say of himself, or of other regenerated persons, that "they are carnal and sold under sin."[54]

Louis Bonnet wrote:

The apostle is speaking here neither of *the natural man* in his state of voluntary ignorance and sin, nor *of the child of God* born anew, set free by grace, and animated by the spirit of Christ, but of the man whose conscience, awakened by the law, has entered sincerely, with fear and trembling, but still *in his own strength,* into the desperate struggle against

---

[54]Macknight, *Commentary,* 92.

evil.[55]

A. T. Robertson, the Southern Baptist's famous Greek scholar, acknowledged the controversy over whether Paul is describing his struggle with sin before or after conversion. Robertson said the words *sold under sin* "seem to turn the scale for the pre-conversion period."[56]

Paul says in v 15 that he does not know what he is doing. This man is double-minded, unstable in all he does (Jas 1:8). The verb γινώσκω (*ginosko*) may mean that he does not understand what is happening. However, it may also carry the implication that he does not like nor approve what is happening. This, according to Arminius, is proof that he is a slave of sin. Although the flesh and Spirit struggle in the life of the regenerate according to Galatians 5:16-17, the fact that his conscience may struggle greatly with his flesh here is no sure indication of his regeneration.[57] His faint desire or inclination toward right is overpowered by passions which "darken the understanding, mislead the judgment, and stupify the conscience," wrote Benson.[58]

Summers wrote that the true evangelical understanding of synergism, the gracious ability to work with God, is that we desire what is right. God works in us both to will and to do of his good pleasure (Phil 2:13). We are not given a desire for the impossible, nor is the desire forced upon us irresistibly.

---

[55]Bonnet, *Épitres de Paul*, 85; quoted by Godet, *Commentary*, 294.

[56]Robertson, *Word Pictures*, 4:369.

[57]Arminius, *Works*, 2:518-521.

[58]Benson, *Notes*, 5:62.

We concur with divine influence.[59] Yet this is not saving grace; it is prevenient or preliminary grace. While unconverted men may approve of the law of God, Benson qualified that approval:

> It is not supposed here that the person spoken of consents at all times to the whole of God's law as good: this inference is limited by what he said in the former verse. Nor is it every evil which he hates, that he does; nor does he always feel that hatred which he mentions against the sins which he commits. He only mentions it as a thing which frequently happened, that the evils which he hated, and was inclined to avoid, were actually committed by him; and the good deeds which his conscience inclined him to do, were not performed. From this he infers, that this inclination implied the consent of his judgment unto the goodness of those laws, which under these circumstances he was in the habit of braking. And, that the minds even of wicked men consent to the law of God as good, is obvious from their approbation of good actions in others.[60]

Although Paul was bound by sin, the problem was not the law but sin's control. His consent that the law is good (v 16) is no indicator of his regeneration because, at the same time he consents, he still continues to serve sin and is condemned by his deeds, which the law disapproves. Commentators frequently refer to an occasion in Trojan mythology when

---

[59]Summers, *Commentary,* 88.

[60]Benson, *Notes*, 5:63.

Media put her two illicit children to death. The Roman poet Ovid, writing in AD 8, has her say,

> I see the right, and I approve it too,
> Condemn the wrong, and yet the wrong pursue.[61]

Jesus told of a son who both consented and rebelled (Matt 21:30). We are all born with a sinful nature, but we each may have a different point of weakness. Hebrews 12:1 refers to our besetting or prevailing sin. Initially we choose to sin, but we also open the door of our life to more than we have chosen. At some point we do not choose to continue the practice of sin, but we continue to sin anyway. What Paul calls "bondage," psychology calls a compulsion, an obsession, or an addiction.

In vv 17-20 Paul describes a sinner who has lost control and continues to sin unwillingly. It is claimed that this person must be regenerate because he has two natures. It is not his new nature which sins, but sin dwelling in him. But this does not prove he is regenerate. Arminius pointed out that the unregenerate also have two principles operating within them: they serve sin, yet consent that the law is good (vv 14-16).[62]

Thus, both the saved and the unsaved have two principles operating. The unsaved have both a conscience which may hold rather high ideals. Yet the unsaved also have a depraved will which desires that which is base and degrading. The saved have the new life of the Spirit and also have the old nature which was passed down from Adam. The determination of true spiritual condition hinges not upon the fact that

---

[61]Ovid, *Metamorphoses*, 7.19-20. This translation by Samuel Garth.

[62]Arminius, *Works*, 2:523-524.

there are two principles present; the true spiritual state is determined by which nature is in control.

It is also argued that the man described in v 17 is regenerated because of the adverbs *now* (νῦν - *nun*) and *no more* (οὐκέτι - *ouketi*). Arminius argued that this division of time marks a distinction before and after Paul was awakened and that is corresponds to v 9. Once Paul was alive without the law, but now he is under the condemnation of the law.[63]

In v 17 ἐνοικέω (*enoikeo*) is a compound verb meaning "to indwell." It is also used in 8:11 of the resurrection hope the regenerate have since they are indwelt by the Spirit. Arminius pointed out the difference between sin existing and sin dwelling. To indwell means to have dominion or to reign.[64] "Sin may exist in the regenerate, but it does not reign in them; it does reign in the unregenerate, even in the awakened. As the demoniac is controlled by the demon that possesses him, so the awakened sinner is controlled by sin, which has taken possession of him," wrote Summers.[65]

In vv 18-19 Paul also speaks both of a desire to do good and the inability of the flesh, or carnal nature, to carry out these good intentions. However, the desire to do right is not sufficient evidence of regeneration. Righteousness reigns in the heart of the regenerate, producing both the will and the power to do right (Phil 2:13).

Fletcher wrote that v 20 describes an awakened, yet carnal, man "who has light enough to see his sinful habits, but not faith and resolution enough to overcome them." When

---

[63] Arminius, *Works*, 2:525-526.

[64] Arminius, *Works*, 2:526-529.

[65] Summers, *Commentary*, 90. See the discussion by Arminius [*Works*, 2:526-529].

Paul was justified, the love of God was shed abroad in his heart (5:5). "He who abides in love abides in God and God in him" (1 John 4:16) and "He who is in you is greater than he who is in the world" (1 John 4:4). Therefore, Fletcher argued, "Now if God dwelt in Paul by his loving Spirit, it becomes our objectors to show that *an indwelling God* and *indwelling sin* are one and the same thing."[66]

Paul testified that the desire to do good was present (v 18), but that evil was also present (v 21). The same word *present* (παράκειμαι - *parakeimai*) is used in both verses; it means to lie beside or to be near. However, the two do not exist in equal proportion. The presence of evil is more powerful and prevails over the presence of a desire to do good.

In v 22 Paul declares that his inner man delights (συνήδομαι - *sunedomai*) in the law of God. This word does not occur anywhere else in the New Testament, although the noun form, ἡδονή (*hedone*), is used. *Hedone* is the basis for the word *hedonism* and carries the concept of pleasure or delight.

Some commentators doubt it could be said that an unbeliever delights or takes pleasure in God's holy law, especially since the unbeliever is hostile toward God (8:7). Sproul declared, "No unregenerate person delights in the law of God in the innermost self. This statement can only be made by a regenerate person, so I am convinced that Paul is speaking of his present condition."[67]

Benson objected that this interpretation is a mere assertion, not inferred from this passage, and is plainly contradicted by the context. The "inner man" does not signify the

---

[66]Fletcher, *Works*, 2:542.

[67]Sproul, *The Glory of God*, 127.

new man. The phrase occurs in 2 Corinthians 4:16 and Ephesians 3:16 and signifies the mind or soul of man, whether or not that mind is under grace.[68] The "inner man" is contrasted with "the outer man" or the physical body. Arminius devoted four pages to an exegesis of these two passages and comes to the same conclusion. He then cited fifteen church fathers and seven contemporary exegetes who supported his interpretation.[69]

Pope said that "the inward man" and "the law of my mind" (vv 22-23) describe the influence of the Holy Spirit to awaken a sense of right, even a desire for it, within a sleeping sinner; yet his nature is still corrupt.[70] Summers wrote that since the Reformers did not have an adequate view of prevenient grace, which operates upon man before regeneration, they stumbled at the declarations in vv 22 and 25.[71]

While Calvin admitted that "the inner man" has a different meaning in 2 Corinthians 4:16, here he insisted that it meant "not simply the soul, but that spiritual part which has been regenerated by God."[72] Yet Rushdoony, an advocate of Calvinism, asked whether the conflict described in v 22 can be true of the unregenerate:

> Over the years, I have had occasions to meet with people who were sometimes in agony over their dilemma. Although unregenerate, they knew the law

---

[68]Benson, *Notes*, 5:64-65.

[69]Arminius, *Works*, 2:548-568.

[70]Pope, *Compendium*, 2:67.

[71]Summers, *Commentary*, 82.

[72]Calvin, *Romans*, 271.

of God in their hearts, and they knew it as the way of life, and sometimes admitted this briefly. On the other hand, because of their sin, they were also suicidal and were at times terrified by their will to death. It is an illusion to believe that the conflict between good and evil exists only in the regenerate, and such an opinion denies the fact of creation by the triune God. . . . The knowledge of God is inescapable for all men, regenerate and unregenerate.[73]

The *inner man* in v 22 "is not the same as *the new man* or *the regenerate* either from the etymology of the word or from the usage of Scripture; and *the inward man* is not peculiar to the regenerate, but...also belongs to the unregenerate," said Arminius.[74] Perhaps the man of Romans 7 delighted in the law until the Holy Spirit convicted him that he was not keeping it. Luke 18:9-14 records the account of a Pharisee who was proud of his keeping of the law, yet he was far from being justified before God. Israel delighted in the law, but did not keep it. To delight in God's law is prevenient grace; to obey God's law is saving grace. The fact that I may appreciate, even be delighted, with great works of art does not, in any sense, make me an artist. Even if I am pleased with God's law, the more important question is whether or not God is pleased with me (8:8).

While he agrees with God's law (v 22), he is under the control of another law (v 23). The Greek language provides two words for *another*: *allos* is another of the same sort; *heteros* denotes another of a different sort. In v 23 Paul uses

---

[73]Rushdoony, *Romans & Galatians*, 119-120.

[74]Arminius, *Works*, 2:547-548.

heteros. The law which Paul was under before his conversion was not the law of God, even though he approved of God's law.

C. K. Barrett interprets vv 22-23 as meaning that although my inner self, the new man or new creation, agrees with God's law, that same law is perverted by my outward man and that produces sin. Barrett disregards this distinction between *allos* and *heteros* in saying that the law which rules in v 23 is evidently the same as God's law which is approved in v 22.

Barrett interprets this whole passage, then, as the Christian's struggle with the present age. The age to come has dawned and the believer has been raised to live a new life. Although the Christian has hope, Paul here describes human nature on earth, not in heaven. Thus, the Christian religion, like other religions, offers hope but no present deliverance.

Barrett also writes that sin produces a counterfeit law which wars upon the true law. Sin has taken possession of the law, made of it a subtle perversion of law; this law is sin. Religion has proven to be a broken reed. Man needs not a law, but deliverance.

Thus, there are two laws. The mind recognizes the law of God, but our human nature recognizes the law which sin has fashioned for this age.[75] Barrett's interpretation here is being influenced more by Karl Barth than by Paul.[76]

While all false religions have created their own legalism which only compounds the problem, and while these perversions of God's law are sin, the basis point made by Paul is simply an elaboration of 6:16-18. There is a present deliver-

---

[75]Barrett, *Commentary*, 149-153.

[76]Dunn, *Word Biblical Commentary*, 38A:397.

ance from sin and it comes not by merely approving God's law, but by yielding to God.

John Stott struggled with his interpretation of "the half-saved," "Old Testament Christian." Because this person loves the law, Stott concluded they were regenerated. Yet they are not a liberated Christian because they are still a slave to sin. Since the indwelling Spirit is the birthright and hallmark of all who belong to Christ (8:9), and since this person knows nothing of the Holy Spirit, they are not a New Testament believer. Stott described the subject as an Old Testament believer, not depicting normal Christianity. He saw vv 4-6, with its contrast of two covenants, as crucial to the interpretation of the rest of the chapter. Stott's interpretation comes close to the Methodist interpretation, but he is hindered primarily by his misunderstanding of the term *delight* in v 22. He interpreted that to mean not only an acknowledgment of the intrinsic goodness of the law, but a love for God's law. Paul never used the word *love* in this chapter and Stott read that meaning into the word *delight*. Stott asked how an unregenerate person, who is hostile to God's law (8:7), declares his delight in it. But 8:7 describes the hostility of a sinful man who is spiritually dead. Romans 7:22 describe an awakened sinner who approves of God's law, but is unable to keep it. Romans 6:18, 22; 8:2 describes a regenerate man who obeys God's law. Thus, Stott wrongly concluded this man, in 7:22, was regenerate.

Stott rejected the two-step paradigm that normal Christian experience passes through Romans 7 into Romans 8; that defeat is a necessary prelude to victory. His analysis sounds similar to the servant/son paradigm of Wesley, yet Wesley taught that servants were not yet regenerate. Stott also sounded like C. Leslie Mitton, who warned against slipping back into legalism. Stott also hesitated to adopt the interpretation of Lloyd-Jones, whom he felt was describing phenomenon of revival, not interpreting the text. Stott, writing in 1994, moved away from his previous position, written in 1966, that "the speaker in the last part of chapter 7 is a mature, believing Christian . . . anyone who acknowledges the spirituality of God's law and his own natural carnality is a Christian of some maturity."[77] Stott now takes a "third position," that the wretched man is neither a regenerate Christian nor unregenerate.[78]

The struggle Paul describes is compared with the struggle depicted in Galatians 5:16-17, but these are not parallel passages. The Galatians passage describes the struggle between the Holy Spirit and the remains of the carnal nature.

Gordon Fee wrote that the differences between Galatians 5:17 and Romans 7:18-20 are far greater than their similarity.[79] Arminius devoted six pages to the distinctions.[80] Summers wrote, "The struggle in Gal 5:17 is very different from that in Romans 7.[81] Lloyd-Jones went so far as to say that Romans 7 says the exact opposite as Galatians 5. One passage describes failure; the other victory.[82] Fee wrote that the phrase "you cannot do the things that you would," in Galatians 5:17, does not contain the slightest hint of inability. Instead, it expresses God's enabling power over against the flesh.[83]

---

[77]Stott, *Men Made New*, 73-74.

[78]Stott, *Romans*, 39; 205-215.

[79]Fee, *God's Empowering Presence*, 435-436.

[80]Arminius, *Works*, 2:568-573.

[81]Summers, *Commentary*, 88.

[82]Lloyd-Jones, *The Law*, 230-232.

[83]Fee, *God's Empowering Presence*, 435.

More recently, Ronald Fung concluded that Galatians 5:17 "refers to a different situation from that envisaged in Rom 7:14ff."[84]

Paul writes the Galatian passage in the second person plural; the Roman passage in the first person singular. In his 1941 commentary on Romans, Anders Nygren claimed that Galatians 5:17 was substantially the same as Romans 7. In his review of Nygren, Leslie Mitton wrote that by omitting from the quotation the words which immediately precede Galatians 5:17,

> Nygren has seriously distorted Paul's meaning. Whereas, v 17, quoted in isolation, sounds a powerful ally to [the position that Romans 7 describes Paul's mature Christian experience], when it is linked with v 16, it can more easily be claimed as support for [the position that Romans 7 describes Paul's pre-conversion experience]. . . . Romans 7 portrays the mastery of the flesh in unaided man, and Gal 5:17 the persisting strength of the flesh in the Christian. But neither declares the mastery of the flesh to be a permanent evil from which there is no deliverance. It is an evil, and an enduring one, but it is one for which an enduring remedy has been supplied. Gal 5:14 offers that remedy. The Christian will still be aware of the continuing strength of the flesh, and of the need for unceasing watchfulness, but he need not any longer "fulfil its promptings." The strong man has been bound by a stronger.[85]

---

[84]Fung, "The Impotence of the Law," 37.

[85]Mitton, "Romans vii. Reconsidered — II," 102.

Here the struggle is between will and conscience. The law tells people what they ought to do, but it is powerless to enable them to do it. What we *want* ultimately wins out over what we *ought*. Greathouse wrote that Augustine brought to Romans 7 the Greek view that this was a struggle between man's reason and his passions; a view cited frequently by Methodist commentators. Greathouse argued instead that Romans 7 depicted the frustration of "anyone who tries to fulfill the demands of God's law without knowing the power of Christ."[86] However, these two interpretations are not necessarily contradictory. The unregenerate, who know what God's law demands, may strive, without knowing the power of Christ, to keep the law. But their sinful desires are so strong that they eventually choose to commit acts of which they intellectually disapprove.

Paul anticipates deliverance from *this body of death* in v 24. Is this a present possibility or a future hope? *This body of death* is figurative language for *the old man*, not the physical body. Passages which speak of Christ's return indicate that he will come for a victorious church, not to rescue carnal "believers." Yet the popular teaching is that deliverance will come when Christ returns to rescue us (8:23; 1 Thess 1:10). Schreiner argues that since the verb *rescue* in v 24 is in the future tense, the rescue from sin will be completed only on the last day.[87] This would lead to the conclusion that the struggle will continue through the Christian life until Christ returns. Wesleyan theology teaches that initial sanctification delivers from the guilt and power of sin. Entire sanctification cleanses the heart from the sin nature. Final sanctification, which

---

[86]Greathouse, *From the Apostles to Wesley*, 70.

[87]Schreiner, *Commentary*, 391.

Christ brings at his return and our resurrection, delivers us from the very presence of sin. Therefore, in one sense Schreiner is right in saying that "the rescue from sin will be *completed* only on the last day." Yet, the present victory over sin, promised in chapter 6, involves more than a transformation which produces "new desires."[88]

R. C. Sproul declared:

> From the day that we are born again, we have to carry around this putrefying, dead, old nature with us, that gets in our way and makes us sick and brings us to all kinds of wicked circumstances. . . . Paul is not saying that there is nothing in the Christian worthy of condemnation. There are plenty of things in my life, even since I have been born again, that deserve condemnation. I continue to sin, and insofar as I continue to sin, what I merit for my sin is the condemnation of God. If God were to judge me right now according to my behavior, I would be condemned. But I have a Savior, and because I am in Christ Jesus, there is no condemnation.[89]

But Paul is asking a rhetorical question, "Who will rescue me?" All that can be implied from this question is that the person asking this question has not yet received deliverance. Paul, at the time he wrote this, had been delivered and gave God thanks for that deliverance in v 25.

This "body of death" (v 24) is the body of sin which causes death. It does not refer to the physical body, but corre-

---

[88]Schreiner, *Commentary*, 301, 337.

[89]Sproul, *The Glory of God*, 128-129.

sponds to "the body of sin" in (6:6). John Murray interpreted the "body of sin" (6:6) and the "body of death" (7:24) as both referring to the physical body.[90] This was also Calvin's position. Notice that 8:2 combines both phrases into "the law of sin and death." There is deliverance from this domination through the new birth. *The Reformation Study Bible* defines "the body of death" as the physical body. Those who experience new life in the Spirit also continue to bear the marks of sin until ultimate deliverance in the resurrection.[91]

While this *body of sin* is a reference to the sinful nature, it cannot be assumed that because the source of the problem is internal that the subject is already regenerate. The new birth breaks the dominion of the sinful nature to the extent that the Christian is no longer in bondage to sin, even though it remains until the point of a fuller deliverance. Leo Cox wrote that we must distinguish between sinfulness in the believer and the state of sinfulness in the unbeliever. While sin remains in the heart of the believer, the believer is no longer a slave to sin. Therefore, it is inconsistent with 1 John 3:9 to reckon the man described here, controlled by a sinful nature and left helpless and wretched under a body of sin, as regenerate.[92]

The deliverance needed must come from outside self. No self-improvement program or positive thinking method will work. There must be confession, repentance, and faith in Christ. Yet the seeker need not wait until the second advent for help to come. Christ will come into the heart of the earnest seeker through his Spirit and bring deliverance from sin.

---

[90]Murray, *NICNT*, 1:220, 268.

[91]Sproul, ed, *Reformation Study Bible*, 1779.

[92]Cox, "Sin in Believers," 28.

Ambrosiaster said that man born in sin is wretched; but, by the grace of God, the human race has been liberated by Christ from this body of death.[93] Therefore, Robert Picirilli's interpretation, that these verses describe the conflict experienced by the normal Christian, is inconsistent with the description given by Paul. Picirilli concluded, "We can only add here that a true Christian is not defeated by that conflict. Nor does he accept living in sin because of it."[94] Yet, vv 14-25 *do* express defeat.

From v 9 to the close of the chapter, Paul uses ἐγώ (*ego*) a total of eight times. While modern psychology has given the term *ego* a specific meaning, that definition should not be imported back to Paul. Since, in the Greek language, the subject is included within the verb, for Paul to restate the subject is to emphasize that the person described is fighting this battle by himself. Paul does not use e*go* in the first six chapters of Romans nor in chapter 8. In contrast the Holy Spirit, who is never mentioned in 7:7-25, is mentioned twenty times in chapter 8. Ironically, Charles Cranfield declared that these verses "depict vividly the inner conflict characteristic of the true Christian, a conflict such as is possible only in the man in whom the Holy Spirit is active, and whose mind is being renewed under the discipline of the gospel."[95]

Some commentators propose the theory that the *I* refers to Adam's experience with God's law in the garden. Such

---

[93] Ambrosiaster, *ACT*, 59-60.

[94] Picirilli, *The Book of Romans*, 134, 138.

[95] Cranfield, *ICC*, 1:340-341.

commentators as Käsemann[96] and Dunn[97] advocated such a parallel. Stott summarized the parallels: Romans 7:9 "once I was alive apart from law" corresponds to the age of innocence in paradise. "The law came" refers to God's command in Gen 2:17 to Adam and Eve not to eat from the forbidden tree. "Sin sprang to life" and seized "the opportunity afforded by the commandment" (Rom 7:8) could mean that sin, in the form of the serpent, was in the garden before man, but had no opportunity until the command have been given by God. Paul's complaint that sin had deceived him (v 11) sounds like Eve's complaint (Gen 3:13). Paul's awakening to his sin was due to the law against covetousness (Rom 7:7) and the sin of Adam and Eve was also due to desire (Gen 3:6). Disobedience to God's command brought death to both Paul (Rom 7:9, 11) and Adam (Gen 2:17; 3:19).[98]

Another view is that the *I* stands for Israel's experience when they received the law at Sinai. Douglas Moo argued that Paul's expression "the coming of the law" would correspond most naturally with the giving of the law at Sinai. Just as Israel had a sense of corporate history, so Paul sees himself in solidarity with Israel.[99]

N. T. Wright took the position that *I* is a rhetorical device, not necessarily Paul's own autobiographical experience. Wright disagreed that *I* refers to Adam, since Romans 5 teaches that the Christian is not in Adam. It is the plight of

---

[96]Käsemann, *Commentary*, 196.

[97]Dunn, *WBC*, 38A:401.

[98]Stott, *Romans*, 200.

[99]Moo, *Romans 1-8*, 453-455.

Israel under the Torah.[100]

However, most commentators opt for the view that the *I* is autobiographical, that Paul is sharing his own experience, and that his own experience is a paradigm for the human race.

In v 25 Paul makes the same point through the use of a double pronoun, "I myself." Pope wrote that αὐτὸς ἐγώ (*autos ego* - I myself) is self without God, in the sense of being without him as its God. He connected v 25 with Ephesians 2:12, which describes the sphere of life and enjoyment that comprise the world of self. "This is the slavery of sin to which man is naturally born, and to which he is naturally predetermined. . . . The mind, the affections, and the will, is fettered and impotent to good. Hence its fallen dignity evermore utters the cry, *O wretched man that I am.*" Yet Haldane, a classic Calvinist commentator, wrote, "This language is suitable only to the regenerate. An unregenerate man is indeed wretched, but he does not feel the wretchedness here expressed."[101]

The application of the law has brought the *I* of this wretched man from a latent state into activity. Though a single personality, v 25 refers both to the mind and the flesh. Yet there is a carnal bias, an outer man, a slave to evil, which is behind even the inner man of reason with his will to good. Although the mind is the nobler faculty, it is in absolute bondage to the flesh, "rendering the will powerless to perform its ineffectual desire." Within the inner man is "the original vice which gives birth to these contradictions." Pope concluded that while "the indwelling sin which the law revealed reduced him to such impotence as could be defined only by death, . .

---

[100]Wright, *NIB*, 10:553, 571.

[101]Haldane, *Exposition*, 298-299.

. there is the state of deliverance *from the law of sin and death* in regeneration."[102]

Mitton argued that the condition described in Romans 7 is true both of the unregenerate and the regenerate whenever we try to live up to the commands of God on our own and left to ourselves. Mitton says this state is true of a man under the law, even if he is nominally a Christian. It can also be true of the converted Christian who has slipped back from daily dependence on the free grace of God into a legalistic attitude. The contrast between Romans 7 and 8, then, is that one man is on his own and the other is "in Christ." However, since the just are to live by faith, even if a person was once justified by faith, the lifestyle of Romans 7 does not come up to justification. It makes little difference whether the person is unregenerate and has not yet been converted or has lost the blessing of regeneration and relapsed.[103]

Wretched is used in v 24 and Revelation 3:17. When Paul cries out in thanks to God in v 25, is he praising God for the condition of bondage he has been describing or because he is now living in a higher state? The groanings of v 24 cannot be connected with the groaning of 8:23. Notice, those who groan in 8:23 have the firstfruits of the Spirit, yet there is not a word about the Spirit after 7:6. Lloyd-Jones also rejected this connection.[104] Sanday and Headlam wrote, "Not until we come to verse 25 is there a single expression which belongs to Christianity."[105]

It seems that in his joy he gets ahead of the story and

---

[102]Pope, *Compendium*, 2:65-67.

[103]Mitton, "Romans vii. Reconsidered — III," 133-135.

[104]Lloyd-Jones, *The Law*, 233-235.

[105]Sanday and Headlam, *ICC*, 186.

rejoices that there is a better way. Then he concludes by restating his argument. However, Packer thinks that if Paul has experienced deliverance from sin, it is very unnatural for him to state that he was still a slave to the law of sin after he had given thanks for his present deliverance from sin.[106] Haldane said that Paul divides himself into two parts, his renewed self and the old man. Thus, he serves both the law of God and the law of sin. "Beyond this no child of God can go while in this world; it will ever remain the character of the regenerate man."[107] Steele and Thomas claim that the entire chapter describes Paul's salvation since he acknowledges Jesus Christ as his Lord in this verse.[108]

Yet this interpretation of v 25 contradicts the whole emphasis of chapters 6-8. Arminius offered a more reasonable interpretation. "In the latter part of the same verse is something resembling a brief recapitulation of all that has been previously spoken." Arminius argued against the interpretation that Paul was partly regenerate and still partly carnal, because the regenerate do not serve the law of God merely through their mind, but through the Spirit.

Pope explained that the exclamation "I thank God through Jesus Christ our Lord!" is a premature earnest or prelude of the greater thanksgiving which fills the next chapter. The preceding words sum up the seventh chapter:

> The "I" of the convicted sinner is awakened to a sense of sin and desire for salvation, but awakened only to find himself struggling in a nature which is

---

[106]Packer, *Keeping in Step with the Spirit*, 144, 163, 267-270.

[107]Haldane, *Exposition*, 299.

[108]Steele and Thomas, *Romans: An Interpretative Outline*, 127.

to him as a body, and so entirely under the bondage of corruption that it might be called a "body of death." This wrestling penitent cries out for his Deliverer: for One whom he knows to be near, and who shall deliver him, not from the body by death, nor from the body as the seat of evil, but from that other self which is as a man of sin within him; One who shall enable him, rescued from the condemnation of the law, to live even in the flesh a sanctified life, free from the law of sin and death. It was this cry which Saul uttered during that ever-memorable time in Damascus; these were the agonies of supplication which his Savior heard when He said, "Behold, he prayeth." The answer he received at once and for ever; the seventh chapter passed into the eighth in his own experience long before he wrote either. He was delivered by one act of his Redeemer from the body of death, inasmuch as his whole being — his spirit and its instrument, his flesh — was inhabited by the Holy Ghost, sin was no longer a necessity of his life; though in the flesh he could please God. He left his Damascus prison with this very song on his lips, and now that he is describing the well-remembered experience, as "a pattern to them that should afterwards believe," he is as it were in haste to tell the secret. Before he has quite ended the narrative of his sore struggles, — when, after conviction but before the new birth, he was only taught that he could not redeem himself, — he greets the coming Deliverer, as it were before the time: "I thank God through Jesus Christ our Lord!"[109]

---

[109] Pope, *The Prayers of St. Paul*, 101-102.

Mention is made of four laws: the law of God, the law of sin, the law of the mind (v 23), the law of the members (v 23). Arminius argued that just as the law of God and the law of sin are direct opposites, so the law of the mind and the law of the members are direct opposites. There are two lords who war against each other — God and sin. Those who are under the law of God have their minds renewed by the Spirit; those under the law of sin commit sin because their members are prisoners to the law of sin. Whichever master we serve is determined by which law we are under. No man can serve two masters. Those who serve Christ have been set free from the law of sin and death (8:2).[110]

Coke summarized the argument: "The law cannot deliver from the body of death; that is, from those carnal appetites, which produce sin, and so bring death; but the grace of God, through Jesus Christ, [which not only give strength to conquer, but] which pardons lapses where there is genuine repentance and faith, delivers us from this body, so that it does not destroy us." Therefore, the conclusion of Romans 8:1 naturally follows.[111] Adam Clarke concluded, "Reader, do not plead for Baal; try, fully try, the efficiency of the blood of the covenant; and be not content with less salvation than God has provided for thee."[112] Sin is treatable; it need not bring eternal damnation.

---

[110]Arminius, *Works*, 2:579-585.

[111]Coke, *Commentary*, 5:78.

[112]Clarke, *Commentary*, 6:93.

Part Three: *Who Is Paul Describing? The Theological Positions*

If the proper interpretation of Romans 7 is a watershed issue, it should not come as a surprise that this chapter is commonly misunderstood. Bernard Ramm called this the most controversial chapter in the entire Scripture in debating the significance of the context.[113] According to the early church fathers, Roman 7 is pre-Christian experience. According to Calvinism, Romans 7 is normal Christianity; according to the Keswick position, it is abnormal Christianity; and according to the Wesleyan-Arminian understanding, it is normal pre-Christian experience.[114]

1. The Patristic Interpretation

Gerald Bray noted:

Most of the Fathers believed that here Paul was adopting the persona of an unregenerate man, not describing his own struggles as a Christian. As far as they were concerned, becoming a Christian would deliver a person from the kind of dilemma the apos-

---

[113]Ramm, *Protestant Biblical Interpretation*, 140.

[114]See Wilder, ed. *Perspectives On Our Struggle With Sin: Three Views of Romans 7*, 2011.

tle is outlining here.[115]

No writer before the fourth century believed Paul was describing the Christian life.[116] Irenaeus (130-202) is the earliest existing writer to comment directly on this passage. He said that Paul's statement, "that there dwells in my flesh no good thing," is typical of human infirmity from which Jesus came to deliver us.[117]

Clement of Alexandria (150-215) explained that when Paul described the war between the law of God and the law of his mind, it was to show that Jesus rescues men from this through salvation.[118]

Tertullian (160-240) taught that the Holy Spirit makes men free from the law of sin and death. After salvation, "Our members, therefore, will no longer be subject to the law of death, because they cease to serve that of sin, from *both* which they have been set free."[119] He also noted that Paul was referring to his pre-Christian days as an unbelieving Jew.[120]

Origen (184-253) wrote:

> Someone who is carnal and sold under sin does not know that the law is spiritual, so how can Paul say

---

[115] Bray, *ACCS*, 189-190.

[116] Jennings, "The Patristic Interpretation of Romans 7:14-25, Part 1-2," 4-7; 3-5.

[117] Irenaeus, *Against Heresies*, 3.20.3. *ANF* 1:450.

[118] Clement of Alexandria, *Stromata*, 3.11:76-78. *ANF* 2:395.

[119] Tertullian, *On the Resurrection of the Flesh*, ch. 46. *ANF* 3:579.

[120] Tertullian, *On Modesty*, ch 17. *ANF* 4:93.

this of himself? In fact, when he says that he is carnal and sold under sin he is playing the part of a teacher of the church by taking on the role of the weak, as he said elsewhere: *I became weak to the weak, so that I might win the weak.*[121]

Methodius of Olympus (260-312) wrote that the expressions:

"That which I do, I allow not," and "what I hate, that do I," are not to be understood of doing evil, but of only thinking it. For it is not in our power to think or not to think of improper things, but to act or not to act upon our thoughts. For we cannot hinder thoughts from coming into our minds, since we receive them when they are inspired into us from without; but we are able to abstain from obeying them and acting upon them. Therefore it is in our power to will not to think these things; but not to bring it about that they shall pass away, so as not to come into the mind again; for this does not lie in our power, as I said; which is the meaning of that statement, "The good that I would, I do not.[122]

Lactantius (250-325) wrote that "it is impossible for a man to be wretched who is endued with virtue."[123]

A third century document called *The Two Epistles Con-*

---

[121]Bray, *ACCS*, 6:190. Origen was quoting 1 Cor 9:22.

[122]Methodius, *The Discourse On the Resurrection*, 3.2. *ANF* 6:371.

[123]Lactantius, *The Divine Institutes*, 3.12; 4.24. *ANF* 7:80; 125.

cerning Virginity, thought to have been written by Clement of Rome, explained that Paul said nothing good dwelt in his flesh "because the Spirit of God is not in it."[124]

Macarius the Egyptian (300-391) said that life in the Spirit was the answer to the life in the flesh which Paul described in Romans 7.[125]

In his comments on Romans 7:23, Cyril of Jerusalem (313-386) taught that the devil had used the flesh against mankind since the time of Adam, but that Jesus in taking upon himself human flesh had saved man's nature.[126]

Basil the Great (330-379) wrote about Paul:

> And after he has developed more fully the idea that it is impossible for one who is in the power of sin to serve the Lord, he plainly states who it is that redeems us from such a tyrannical dominion in the words: "Unhappy man that I am, who shall deliver me from the body of this death? I give thanks to God through Jesus Christ our Lord." Further one, he adds: "There is now, therefore no condemnation to them that are in Christ Jesus, who walk not according to the flesh.[127]

In his rebuttal of Eunomius, an Arian theologian, Gregory of Nyssa (335-395) said that when we were held by death and sold under sin, Jesus Christ took upon himself the form of a

---

[124]Clement of Rome, *First Epistle*, ch. 8. *ANF* 8:57-58.

[125]Macarius, *Fifty Spiritual Homilies of St. Macarius the Egyptian*, 7.

[126]Cyril, *Catechetical Lectures*, Lecture 12:15. *NPNF*2 7:75.

[127]Basil, *Concerning Baptism*, 343.

servant; in his incarnation he redeemed up from death and delivered our souls.[128]

Paulinus of Nola (354-431) believed that Romans 7 was the picture of a man in his pre-Christian days.

> For now the old war, in which the law of sin struggled with the law of God, is wiped out in Christ, for the spirit which serves God governs by faith the soul subjected to it, and the flesh in turn becomes the servant of the soul, accompanying it, as it serves God, in every duty of obedience.[129]

John Chrysostom (347-407) was very insistent that the flesh is not inherently evil. He explained:

> Paul met the difficulty posed by postbaptismal sin by saying that it is due to our laziness. For now that we are in Christ Jesus we have the power to avoid walking after the flesh, but before that it was a difficult task.[130]

In the fourth and fifth centuries, there were four men who paved the way for a new understanding of Romans 7. Gregory of Nazianzen (329-390) understood that Roman 7 described a believer who "by a long course of philosophic training, and gradual separation of the noble and enlightened part of the soul from that which is debased and yoked with darkness, or

---

[128] Gregory of Nyssa, *Against Eunomius*, 2:3. *NPNF*2 5:104.

[129] Paulinus, *Letter* 12.6; *Letters of St. Paulinus of Nola*, 1:111.

[130] Bray, *ACCS*, 6:200; Chrysostom, *The Epistle to the Romans*, Homily 13, *NPNF*1 11:431.

by the mercy of God, or by both together, and by a constant practice of looking upward" could overcome the desires of the flesh presented in Romans 7.[131]

Ambrose (340-397) understood Romans 7 as pre-Christian experience until AD 394 when he wrote, "Well, we who are older sin, too. In us, too, the law of this flesh wars against the law of our mind, and makes us captives of sin, so that we do what we would not."[132]

Augustine (354-430) originally believed Romans 7 referred to Paul before his salvation. "But afterwards I was constrained to give up the idea."[133] However, what he embraced was the explanation of Methodius that Paul was describing evil desires, not evil actions. Augustine wrote:

> Though his carnal desire still exist, the man who is renewed by grace by not giving into sin does not serve them. With his mind he serves the law of God, even though with his flesh he serves the law of sin. Paul calls the law of sin the mortal condition which stems from the transgression of Adam, because of which we are born mortal. It is because the flesh has fallen that the lusts of the flesh entice us. . . .
> These are the words of one who is now under grace but still battling against his own lust, not so that he consents and sins but so that he experiences desires

---

[131]Gregory of Nazianzen, *In Defense of His Flight to Pontus*, §91. *NPNF2* 7:222-223.

[132]Ambrose, *Concerning Repentance*, 2:8, §74. *NPNF2* 10:355.

[133]Augustine, *Against Two Letters of the Pelagians*, 1:22. *NPNF1* 5:384.

which he resists.[134]

Not until Jerome (347-420) did anyone attempt to use Romans 7 to justify his personal behavior.

> For we do not what we would but what we would not; the soul desires to do one thing, the flesh is compelled to do another. If any persons are called righteous in scripture . . . they are called righteous according to that righteousness mentioned in the passage I have quoted: "A just man falls seven times and rises up again," . . . Zachariah the father of John who is described as a righteous man sinned in disbelieving the message sent to him and was at once punished with dumbness. Even Job, who at the outset of his history is spoken of as perfect and upright and uncomplaining, is afterwards proved to be a sinner both by God's words and by his own confession.[135]

Jerome confessed, "Yet, to lay bare my own weakness, I know that I wish to do many things which O ought to do and *yet cannot*. For while my spirit is strong and leads me to life my flesh *is weak and draws me to death*."[136]

Craig Keener wrote that the majority of scholars today contend that Romans 7:14-25 cannot refer to the Christian

---

[134]Bray, *ACCS*, 6:199.

[135]Jerome, *Letter* to Rusticus, Letter 122, §3. *NPNF*2 6:228-229.

[136]Jerome, *Letter* to Ctesiphon, Letter 133, §9. *NPNF*2 6:278.

life.[137] Caleb Friedeman concluded,

> Modern New Testament scholarship has largely seconded this early Christian consensus. . . . Of course, this ancient and modern consensus does not settle the matter; majority views can be wrong. But it should make us question whether it is self-evident that Paul is speaking about his Christian experience in Romans 7:14-25. It should also make us ask what these church fathers and New Testament scholars are seeing that so many of us do not.[138]

2. The Calvinistic Interpretation

Most of the reformers believed that when Paul was describing his struggles with sin, he is speaking of himself as a regenerate person. However, there were a few dissenting voices, such as Arminius and Sozzini.[139]

Those who follow the emphasis of Augustine teach that Romans 7 was the present experience of Paul at the time of writing. For Augustine this was the highest state of Christian experience in this life. He stated, "No one in this life can be so privileged that there should not be in his members a law fighting against the law of his mind."[140]

Martin Luther declared that man is at the same time just

---

[137] Keener, *The Mind of the Spirit*, 58.

[138] Ayars, Bounds, and Friedeman, *Holiness*, 133.

[139] Adams, *Reformation Commentary on Scripture*, 8:386. Fausto Sozzini or Socinus (Latin), however, was heretical.

[140] Augustine, *Retractions*, 1.19; quoted by Flew, *Idea of Perfection*, 208.

and yet sinful (*simul justus est et peccat*).[141] Luther said:

> A Christian is therefore both a sinner and a saint; he is evil and is good. In ourselves we are sinners, but Christ gives us another name when He mercifully forgives our sins for His sake. Hence both appellations are true. Sins are yet in us, for the old Adam still lives within; and again they are not present, because God blots them out for Christ's sake. They are present before my eyes; I see them and I feel them; but there stands Christ and tells me to repent, to confess myself just what I am, a sinner, and declares unto me forgiveness of my sins through faith in His name. Repentance alone, though necessary, is not sufficient; faith in the remission of sins through Christ must also be added. Where there is such faith, God no longer sees sin; for then we appear before Him not in our own righteousness, but in that of Christ.[142]

In other words we are at the same time sinner and saint, always repenting.[143] In his *Institutes of the Christian Religion*, Calvin wrote:

> Paul takes his example from a regenerated man, that is, himself. He therefore says that he is held bound in miserable bondage, so that he cannot consecrate

---

[141]Luther, *Romans*, 98-99.

[142]Luther, *House-Postil*, 2:303.

[143]It was irresponsible for Outler to claim this is identical with Wesley's teaching, as he did in Wesley, *BE Works*, 1:323.

himself wholly to obedience to the divine law. Hence, he is compelled to exclaim with groaning: "Wretched man that I am! Who will deliver me from this body subject to death?"[144]

In his commentary on Romans 7:24, Calvin wrote, "Paul, by his own example stimulates [the most perfect] to anxious groanings, and bids them, as long as they sojourn on earth, to desire death, as the only true remedy to their evils."[145]

John Calvin followed Augustine in teaching "that sin always exists in the saints until they are divested of the mortal body." Calvin also taught, "As long as we inhabit the prison of our body we shall have to maintain an incessant conflict with the vices of our corrupt nature."[146] Sutcliffe summarized Calvin's teaching that "our old man, the man of sin, goes down to the grave with the body, but does not rise with it in the resurrection." Sutcliffe concluded, "If it be true that the grave purifies the deceased from the old man, then sin has its seat in the body; whereas the scriptures place it in the mind. If the Father, and the Son, with the Comforter, make his abode with us, how can we be carnal, and like Ahab, sold under sin!"[147]

In 1668 John Owen wrote *The Nature, Power, Deceit, and Prevalency of the Remainders of Indwelling Sin in Believers*. He began the book by assuming that Paul described

---

[144]Calvin, *Institutes of the Christian Religion*, McNeill ed, 2:1313. While there have been several translations of Calvin, regardless of the edition, see 4.15.12. See also 2.7.5 and 3.9.4.

[145]Calvin, *Romans*, 273.

[146]Greathouse, *From the Apostles to Wesley*, 94-95.

[147]Sutcliffe, *Commentary*, 2:457.

himself and the condition of all who are regenerate in Romans 7. Two laws operate within the regenerate: the law of the Spirit of life *and* the law of sin. Although the law of sin has its rule broken and its strength weakened, yet it is still a law of great force and power. Anyone who contends against it shall know and find that it is present with them, that it is powerful in them. While this law remains *in* the believer, it is not *to* them, as it is to unbelievers.

Owen wrote that if grace is maintained in the believer, the will to do good prevails against the power of indwelling sin. But the believers *worst* condition, unwilling sin, is better than the sinners *best* condition, which is willing sin. Yet the law of sin dwells in the heart of the believer, where it maintains a rebellion against God all our days. Sometimes it has more strength, sometimes less; but it is always in rebellion as long as we live and may bring us into captivity, causing us to sin against our will. Since we carry in us all our days this enmity against God, we must be on guard constantly.

Owen admitted that a believer might be led captive for a season by some particular sin. It may have power over him as it seems to have done with many Old Testament saints, but after awhile the desire to be freed from the law of sin will produce a sigh and cry for deliverance. While God may even take the life of an unbeliever to stop the progress of his sin, God does not judicially cut off and take away the life of any who are his.[148]

Charles Hodge declared at v 14, "There is no believer, however advanced in holiness, who cannot adopt the language

---

[148]Owen, *Works*, 6:157-322. I have summarized this section. Ryle's 1877 book, *Holiness: Its Nature, Hindrances, Difficulties, and Roots*, would present the believer's state in much the same way.

here used by the apostle."[149] Robert Haldane stated:

> By thus describing his inward conflict with sin, and showing how far short he came of the demands of the law, he proves the necessity of being dead to the law as a covenant, since, in the highest attainments of grace during this mortal life, the old nature, which he calls flesh, still remains in believers. At the same time he represents himself as delighting in the law of God, as hating sin, and looking forward with confidence to future deliverance from its power.[150]

B. B. Warfield labeled the teaching of the Reformers "miserable-sinner Christianity." Warfield defended this view saying, "Though blessed with every spiritual blessing in the heavenlies in Christ, we are still in ourselves just 'miserable sinners': 'miserable sinners' saved by grace to be sure, but 'miserable sinners' still." Thus the believer continues to sin, recognize his sinfulness, live a life of unbroken penitence, and yet rest assured of God's love.[151]

Steele and Thomas wrote that whether Romans 7:14-25 describes Paul's experience *before* or *after* his conversion is a vital question. If this was descriptive of Paul's pre-Christian experience, then the passage has no bearing on the nature of

---

[149]Hodge, *Commentary*, 229. Incredibly, Brown, advocating the holiness position, agreed with Hodge [*The Meaning of Sanctification*, 25, 27, 29, 64].

[150]Haldane, *Exposition*, 277.

[151]Warfield, *Perfectionism*, 1:113-132. Packer referred to Warfield's statement with approval [*Keeping in Step with the Spirit*, 123-124].

the Christian life. They assert that this describes Paul's experience as a mature Christian and that sanctification is never perfected in this life. In this discussion they include a statement from Charles Spurgeon:

> If God were ever to allow the fountains of the great deeps of depravity to break up in the best man that lives, he would make as bad a devil as the Devil himself is. . . . There is tinder enough in the saint who is nearest to heaven to kindle another hell if God should but permit a spark to fall upon it. In the very best of men, there is an infernal and well-nigh infinite depth of depravity.[152]

James Montgomery Boice also concluded that Romans 7 described the mature Christian.[153] *The Reformation Study Bible* surveyed four possible interpretations, concluding the most probable is that "Paul is describing himself and Christians generally who, although in Christ and free from the condemnations of the law, do not yet perfectly fulfill the requirements of the law. . . . Paul is actually describing a profound conflict that every Christian finds inherent in his life in Christ: Christ dwells in him, yet sin also dwells in him. Perfect conformity to God's will is at present out of his reach."[154] John MacArthur claimed that "Paul is here describing the most spiritual and mature of Christians."[155]

---

[152] Steele and Thomas, *Romans*, 126-130.

[153] Boice, *Romans*, 2:763-770.

[154] Sproul, ed. *The Reformation Study Bible*, 1778.

[155] MacArthur, *Romans 1-8*, 379.

3. *The Keswick/Dispensational Interpretation*

The Keswick interpretation is also the concurrent theory, that the saint is living in Romans 7 and 8 at the same time. C. I. Scofield wrote that Romans 7:15-25 personifies the struggle of the two natures within the believer.[156]

> Romans 7 is a record of the conflict of the regenerate man with his old self, and is, therefore, intensely personal. "I would," "I do not," "I would not," "I do," is the sad confession of defeat which finds an echo in so many Christian hearts. In the eighth chapter the conflict still goes on, but how blessedly impersonal! There is no agony, for Paul is out of it; the conflict is now between "flesh"— Saul of Tarsus — and the Holy Spirit. Paul is at peace and victorious.[157]

Lewis Sperry Chafer, a disciple of Scofield, developed this two-natures theory. He taught that regeneration was the addition of a new nature rather than the re-creation of the old. He said the new nature was possessed in conjunction with the old nature so long as we are in this body. "The presence of two opposing natures in one individual results in conflict."[158] Chafer taught that the believer would make progress little by little as the new nature counteracted the old.

John MacArthur wrote that when Chafer's book *He That*

---

[156]*The New Scofield Reference Bible*, 1219.

[157]*The New Scofield Reference Bible*, 1219; Scofield, *Rightly Dividing the Word of Truth*, 58.

[158]Chafer, *He That Is Spiritual*, 142.

Is Spiritual was first published in 1918, it was extremely controversial. "Prior to this century, no serious theologian would have entertained the notion that it is possible to be saved yet see nothing of the outworking of regeneration in one's life-style or behavior." MacArthur went on to say that Chafer's concept of two classes of Christians, carnal and spiritual, "was a foreign concept to most Christians in Dr. Chafer's generation, but it has become a central premise for a large segment of the church today." It "became the basis for a whole new way of looking at the gospel."[159]

Chafer asserted that grace is rendered ineffectual if we preach that a sinner must surrender to God. He labeled it an error of the first magnitude to require the unregenerate to surrender to the Lordship of Christ. He also said it creates confusion to demand that the unsaved must dedicate themselves to God's will in their daily lives as an added condition. He said this was an Arminian notion that the unregenerate are even able to dedicate their lives to God through common or uncommon grace. As a theologian, Chafer knew the proper term was "prevenient grace." This is the grace which precedes the human response of faith enabling a sinner to repent and believe.

Chafer taught that all gospel preaching should avoid the life to be lived beyond regeneration. When believers are taught that they may voluntarily dedicate their lives to God, the preacher must remind the unsaved repeatedly that issues of Christian character, conduct, and service have no application to them. Nor should sinners be exhorted to confess sin, make restitution, or seek God. All that was necessary was to believe. Chafer admonished preachers to preach the Lordship of Christ exclusively to Christians and the Saviorhood of

---

[159]MacArthur, *The Gospel According to Jesus*, 23-25.

Christ to the unsaved.[160]

Chafer said that a Christian is a Christian because he is rightly related to Christ, but "he that is spiritual" is spiritual because he is rightly related to the Spirit, in addition to his relation to Christ in salvation.[161] While Chafer acknowledges that all Christians are baptized with the Spirit, he says not all are Spirit-filled. Chafer gave seven manifestations of the Spirit which he says are experienced only by the higher class of Christians, the Spirit-filled believer.[162]

In the second century, Irenaeus wrote in *Against Heresies* against the three stages of fleshly, soulish, and spiritual persons, calling this teaching a gnostic heresy. While we may talk of our flesh, our soul, or our spirit, a human being consists of all three together. They do not designate types of persons. Irenaeus probably would have also rejected the modern distinction between carnal Christians and Spirit-filled Christians.[163]

The description Chafer gave of the "Spirit-Filled Life" is the biblical description of regeneration. According to Chafer, the seven marks of the Spirit-filled are as follows:

- Christian character produced by the Spirit. A carnal Christian may not exhibit any spiritual fruit. Chafer wrote elsewhere that the fruit of the Spirit is the experience of every believer *who comes into right adjustment*

---

[160]Chafer, *Systematic Theology*, 3:372-389.

[161]Chafer, *He That Is Spiritual*, 15.

[162]Chafer, *He That Is Spiritual*, 45.

[163]See also Graham, "Are There Carnal Christians?"

with the Spirit.[164] However, the fruit of the Spirit is characteristic of all believers. John Wesley taught that this was the indirect witness that one was actually born again.
- Christian service.
- Taught by the Spirit.
- Praise promoted by the Spirit.
- Led by the Spirit. Yet Paul taught that those who were led by the Spirit are the sons of God (Rom 8:14). Paul makes no such distinction between two classes of Christians as Chafer did.
- Witness of the Spirit. Again, in Romans 8:16 Paul teaches that the Spirit testifies that we are God's children. There is no fine print limiting this promise to only the Spirit-filled.
- Intercession of the Spirit. But again, the Spirit leads all true Christians to pray and assists them in prayer.[165]

There are not two kinds of Christians, carnal and spiritual. If we are double-minded in our thinking, we will be contradictory in our preaching. This two-natures theory, as developed by Chafer, is one of the major reasons for lawlessness in the church today. B. B. Warfield expressed his exasperation with this teaching.

> It is not only hard for a fallen man to be good, we are told, but impossible. This is not altered by his "new birth." The "new birth" does not change his "fallen nature." It only put into him, by its side, a "new nature." Henceforth he has two natures in him,

---

[164]Chafer, *Grace*, 338. Italics added.

[165]Chafer, *He That Is Spiritual*, 39-81.

one of which can only sin, and the other of which cannot sin. The man himself . . .sits up between these two natures and turns over the lever as he lists, to give the one nature or the other momentary control. The two natures, we are told, have absolutely no effect on one another. . . . At any rate it belongs ineradicably to "the Christian" to turn on the old carnal nature, or the new Spiritual nature, as he may choose, and let it act for him. Who this "Christian" is who possesses this power it is a little puzzling to make out. He cannot be the old carnal nature, for that old carnal nature cannot do anything good — and presumably, therefore would never turn on the Spirit in control. He cannot be the new Spiritual nature, for this new Spiritual nature cannot do anything evil — and this "Christian" "may choose to walk after the flesh." Is he possibly some third nature? We hope not, because two absolutely antagonistic and noncommunicating natures seem enough to be in one man. The only alternative seems, however, to be that he is no nature at all — just a nonentity: and then we do not see how he can turn on anything.[166]

John Wesley taught that sin remained but did not reign in the believer.[167] However, Chafer claimed a believer could be a new creation and yet remain a carnal Christian without any change in character. He stated that the carnal Christian is also

---

[166]Warfield, *Perfectionism*, 2:585-586.

[167]Wesley, "Salvation by Faith," 2.6; "On Sin in Believers," 1.6; "The Repentance of Believers," 1.2; "The Scripture Way of Salvation," 3.6.

characterized by a walk that is on the same plane as that of the natural man.[168] Yet Romans 6 asserts that justification and initial sanctification are bound together, and we cannot have the one without having the other. Randall Gleason wrote that Chafer overemphasized the discontinuity between justification and sanctification and underestimated the transforming power of regeneration. "To imagine that a person can be justified without any change for the better in his condition demonstrates a deficient view of both justification and sanctification."[169]

It is both an inconsistency to teach that one can become born again without any change and an inconsistency to teach that a believer can switch back and forth between the old lifestyle and the new. When the victory over sin, taught in Romans 6, has been redefined as victory over the guilt and not the power of sin, as a positional victory but not a practical one, as a theory we *reckon* to be true in the face of evidence to the contrary; when the victory over sin described is an experience of sanctification beyond the new birth — we should not be surprised that the defeat expressed in this chapter is somehow made compatible with the victory over sin taught in the previous chapter.

Barnhouse explained that while Paul was regenerate, he had not yet learned to overcome sin. Yet elsewhere he wrote that the great conflict of this chapter is the conflict of the believer in the most advanced stages of his spiritual experience.[170] One the one hand, Barnhouse asserted that a profess-

---

[168] Chafer, *He That Is Spiritual*, 12.

[169] Gleason, "B. B. Warfield and Lewis S. Chafer on Sanctification," 241-256.

[170] Barnhouse, *Romans*, 7:30.

ing Christian who habitually practices sin cannot be regenerate; on the other hand, he believes the true Christian will always fall short because of indwelling sin "which no watchfulness can avoid, no prayerfulness can prevent, no faith can turn aside." Apparently the state of "no condemnation" does not result from deliverance from sin, but sanctification is a paradigm shift regarding sin.

Barnhouse explained that many Christians go through an experience like Paul's because of false teaching that where there is sin there is no salvation. They lose their joy until they can get free from the law. While Paul called himself "carnal," he "doubtless saw signs of spiritual growth within himself and in some fields where he had been defeated he was now victorious. . . . A spiritual man would know himself so well that he would consider himself carnal." But while Paul calls himself "carnal," we would call him "spiritual."[171]

William Newell declared, "The believer is not under law, not under external enactments, not under conditions; but he has already an eternal standing in grace, — that is, in already secured Divine favor, by a sovereign act of God; which has not only reckoned to him Christ's atoning work, but has placed him fully in the place of Christ's present acceptance with God!" Newell insisted not only that gentiles were never under Mosaic law; but that, according to v 14, we are not under any law, "though doubtless all men have moral responsibility." Newell interpreted 10:4 to mean that "the Law is no more a rule of life than it is a means of righteousness. Walking in the Spirit has now taken the place of walking by ordinances." Therefore, Newell saw the way for the Christian to get out of Romans 7 is to realize he is not under law, but

---

[171]Barnhouse, *Romans*, 5:223-254.

under grace.[172] Thus, the believer's problem is not with sin, but with the law. Deliverance is not freedom from sin, but the antinomian rationalization (which he mistakes for faith) that since we are unconditionally secure, neither the law nor sin matters.

Ronald Fung argued that Romans 7:14-25 may best be understood as the state of a Christian who lives under law, as an illustration that the law cannot overcome indwelling sin or release from its bondage. Thus, a carnal Christian is immature and does not yet know how to live by the Spirit. Fung admitted the difficulty created by this interpretation; that v 24 is the cry of the Christian and v 25a involves a change of speaker to the apostle Paul. But this interjection is not the greatest difficulty. How can this description of a carnal Christian square with 6:14? Fung argues that in 6:14 Paul means that all Christians are freed from the law as a rule of life. As carnal Christians, they are no longer condemned for the same practices that brought condemnation prior to their conversion because they are now under grace, not law. Fung resorted to an antinomian position that, while believers may be defeated by fleshly desires, their victory comes by walking in the Spirit, not through the legalism of keeping the law. Therefore, Paul's purpose is to show that the law is powerless to sanctify the Christian.[173]

John Walvoord wrote on sanctification from an "Augustinian-Dispensational" perspective. This label is misleading since Walvoord advocates the two-nature view of Chafer. This position has little to do with dispensational distinctives or with Augustine who taught the believer could

---

[172]Newell, *Romans Verse by Verse*, 235, 231-234, 393, 281-283.

[173]Fung, "The Impotence of the Law," 40-46.

not get beyond the Romans 7 struggle. MacArthur says Chafer's concept of two classes of believers is an example of dispensationalism's methodology carried too far. "There is a tendency, however, for dispensationalists to get carried away with compartmentalizing truth to the point that they can make unbiblical distinctions. An almost obsessive desire to categorize everything neatly has led various dispensationalist interpreters to draw hard lines not only between the church and Israel, but also between salvation and discipleship, the church and the kingdom, Christ's preaching and the apostolic message, faith and repentance, and the age of law and the age of grace."[174]

Anthony Hoekema said the basic problem with the two-natures position, as stated by Walvoord, was that

> he fails to do full justice to the fact that a decisive break with sin was brought about by Christ for believers — so that sin, though still present in the believer, no longer has dominion — and to the amazing truth that the believer is now indeed, a new creature, old things having passed away.... He gives the impression that the Christian is something like a spiritual seesaw with two contradictory types of inner tendencies. With both tugging at one's heart, a believer can go either way.[175]

Robert Shank asserts that the believer is a single spiritual entity; and whatever he does, he does as a whole man.[176] John

---

[174]MacArthur, *The Gospel According to Jesus*, 25.

[175]Hoekema, "Response to Walvoord," 231.

[176]Shank, *Life in the Son*, 212-216.

Murray wrote in *Principles of Conduct,* "The believer is both old man and new man; when he does well he is acting in terms of the new man which he is; when he sins he is acting in terms of the old man which he also still is. This interpretation does not find support in Paul's teaching. . . . The old man is the unregenerate man; the new man is the regenerate man created in Christ Jesus unto good works. It is no more feasible to call the believer a new man and an old man, than it is to call him a regenerate man and an unregenerate. . . . Our old man has been crucified."[177]

Henry Brockett wrote that Romans 6 and 8 were concurrent, but that Romans 7 was not concurrent with chapter 8. "Romans 6 is normal New Testament Christian experience, but some teachers insist that Romans 7 is concurrent Christian experience. But can they explain how one can be free from sin and in bondage to sin at the same time?" Brockett pointed out, in an overview of the book of Romans, that Paul stops periodically to look back. Therefore, it is not necessary to interpret Romans 7 as concurrent.[178]

4. The Wesleyan-Arminian Interpretation

The Wesleyan-Arminian interpretation has always been that Romans 7 is *not* describing the experience of someone who is saved. *A Dissertation on the True and Genuine Sense of the Seventh Chapter of the Epistle to the Romans* by James Arminius was published in 1613. Arminius lived from 1560-1609. This dissertation was published after his death by the nine orphan children of Arminius, who stated that Arminius

---

[177]Murray, *Principles of Conduct,* 211-218.

[178]Brockett, *The Christian and Romans 7,* 15-24, 54.

had been revising the manuscript for publication when he died.[179]

M. B. Riddle wrote, "The Arminian controversy really began upon the exegesis of this passage."[180] This was his first public break with Calvinism, which had unanimously understood vv 14-25 as depicting the heart of every Christian believer.[181] As editor of Calvin's *Institutes*, John T. McNeill added a footnote to Calvin's interpretation of Romans 7:24, "This is the cardinal point at which Arminius departed from Calvin."[182]

While Arminius has continued to be maligned to this day, his dissertation has never been refuted. This dissertation runs over 200 pages. Arminius argued that Paul is not speaking about himself, nor about a man living under grace; but he has transferred to himself the person of a man placed under the law. While Paul writes in the first person, he cannot be speaking of himself because what he ascribes to himself in this chapter is at variance with what he writes about himself elsewhere.

A regenerate man has a mind freed from the darkness and vanity of the world and illuminated with the true and saving knowledge of Christ and with faith. He has been delivered from the dominion and slavery of sin. He has put off the old man and put on the new man. His desires conform to the will of God, not to please the flesh. He has received the Spirit; and through the Holy Spirit he has victory over sin, the world, and

---

[179]Bangs, *Arminius*, 186.

[180]*Lange's Commentary*, 5:245.

[181]McGonigle, *Sufficient Saving Grace,* 22.

[182]McNeill, ed. *Institutes*, 2:1312. See also Stanglin and McCall, *Jacob Arminius*, 161-162.

Satan. He actually desists from evil and does good. However, he must grow in grace; for sometimes he stumbles, falls, wanders astray, commits sin, and grieves the Holy Spirit. Yet, this is not the pattern of his life.

The unregenerate man may be blind and ignorant of the will of God. He may sin without any remorse of conscience or fear of God. But the unregenerate are also those who do not do the will of God, even when they know it. They know the way of righteousness, but depart from it. God's law is written upon their conscience. They may receive the truth and even come to baptism, but they did not die to the old man and were not raised to life as a new man.

From 6:12-14 Arminius concluded that Christians are not under the law, but under grace. While sin has dominion over those who are under the law, sin shall not have dominion over those who are under grace. When Paul uses the phrase "under the law" (6:14), he describes a sinner under the guilt and condemnation of the law. Those who are "without law" (v 9) do not have the written law, but are still under the authority of God's moral law.

Coke declared, "The moral law is truth, everlasting and unchangeable, and therefore, as such, can never be abrogated." Therefore, when we are said to be released from the law (v 6), Coke gave three respects in which the law was abolished: as civil law pertaining to the Jewish nation, as types and figures which anticipated the gospel, and as the administration of death, which subjected transgressors to its curse and condemnation without affording any hope or remedy.[183]

Those who are "under grace" are under the law of Christ. However, to be under grace is the opposite of being under law

---

[183]Coke, *Commentary*, 5:74-75.

because those under grace are free from the guilt and condemnation of the law. Those under grace have been endowed with the Spirit of adoption and regeneration.

Arminius then shows the connection between chapter 6 and chapter 7. That we are not under law, but grace is illustrated in 7:1-4. The proposition that sin has dominion over those under the law is picked up in 7:5 and the opposite condition, that sin does not have dominion over those under grace, agrees with 7:6.

Paul then returns to the proposition that sin has dominion over those who are under the law. This proposition is expanded upon in 7:7-14. In this section he uses the first person to describe the condition introduced in v 5, "When we were in the flesh." The law is neither sin nor the cause of sin. The law serves as the indicator of sin. Sin is the reason for condemnation.

From v 14 to the end of this chapter, Paul now gives two reasons for sin: the man under the law is carnal and he is under the dominion of sin. The slavery of sin is described in v 15. Paul draws from this description two consequences: the sinner is unable to keep God's law and the sinner is under the control of sin. Carl Bangs concluded, "It is inappropriate, then, to contrast Arminius' theology with other Reformed theology in terms of 'free will.' Arminius agrees that there is no 'free will' in the life of sin."[184] Clarke wrote:

> The plain state of the case is this: the soul is so completely fallen, that it has no *power* to do *good* till it receive that power from on high. But it has power to *see* good, to *distinguish* between *that* and *evil*; to *acknowledge* the excellence of this good, and to *will*

---

[184]Bangs, *Arminius*, 191.

it, from a conviction of that excellence; but *farther* it cannot go.

Clarke concluded that, while Satan cannot force us to sin against our will, we can do no good unless we receive grace from God.[185] In v 18 Paul returns to the cause of condemnation. The law is unable to break the power of sin in a man who is under the law. Paul repeats his previous conclusion: the sinner is under the control of sin. Therefore, the sinner is under the law of sin. Verse 21 comes back to the proposition of v 14. But he goes on in vv 22-23 to prove the conclusion he has just stated. A man who is under the law cannot have dominion over sin. Whether willingly or unwillingly, such a person is compelled to fulfill the lusts of sin. The chapter closes with a cry for deliverance from the dominion of sin and an exclamation of thanksgiving that there is deliverance through Jesus Christ. Then Paul reduces his argument to a single sentence: he is under the law and a slave to sin.

Arminius then argued that the opening verses of chapter 8 confirm his interpretation. The *therefore* of 8:1 is a conclusion. The first five chapters treated righteousness and remission of sins. Chapters 6-7 dealt with the power to conquer sin and live in a holy manner. Those who are in Christ Jesus do not walk in the condemnation of the law and under the dominion of sin.

After devoting over a hundred pages to exegesis, Arminius then cited fourteen ancient church fathers, several writers of the middle ages, and seven contemporary commentators who all agreed with his interpretation. Arminius asserted that none of the ancient doctors of the church approved of the opposite interpretation.

---

[185]Clarke, *Commentary*, 6:89.

Augustine originally took the same position as Arminius in his *Exposition of Certain Propositions in the Epistle to the Romans* and in his book addressed to Simplicianus, Bishop of Milan. Augustine made two assertions: that this chapter must be understood as relating to a man under the law and that this chapter must not be understood as relating to a man under grace. Augustine over-reacted to the Pelagian heresy, which taught the perfectibility of human nature through the exercise of human will, and retracted his original position. It was while Augustine was involved in the Pelagian debate that he reinterpreted Romans 7 to be the highest state of Christian experience.[186]

In his debate with Pelagius, Augustine later retracted the second position, but never denied the first. In other words, he applied the chapter to both categories. However, when Augustine allowed that this chapter might apply to the regenerate, he interpreted it as describing concupiscence or sexual lust and not the actual commitment of sin by the regenerate. By reducing original sin to sexual desire, Augustine perpetuated the Greek concept that the human body is sinful. By viewing all sexual desire as sin, Augustine made popular the view that this struggle, described in Romans 7, would continue until death, even in the regenerate.

Arminius objected to this interpretation by Augustine which reduces sin to sexual desire. "I beseech St. Augustine to point out to me a single passage of Scripture, in which the regenerate are called *carnal* because they still have within them the lusts of the flesh."

Arminius argued that his interpretation is not heretical nor is it associated with Pelagius, who denied that the corruption which came because of the fall destroyed the power of

---

[186]Greathouse, *From the Apostles to Wesley*, 68.

men to conform themselves to the law of God. The argument of Pelegius was that the man of Romans 7 had the ability to will a right relationship with God. It was to refute this heresy that Augustine was "unwilling to ascribe to the natural man even this powerless longing after higher and better things."[187] Those who followed him would claim that man could not choose right *even after* regeneration. Although the Wesleyan-Arminian view is frequently maligned as "semi-Pelegian," the argument of Arminius is that Romans 7 depicts the inability of the unregenerate.

Arminius opposed, as an injurious interpretation, the view that this chapter deals with a man who is regenerate and under grace. The Scriptures ascribe to divine grace in the regenerate, not only to *will* but also to *do* (Phil 2:13). Through the grace of God, our old man is crucified that we should not serve sin (6:6). Grace enables us, through the help of the Spirit, to put to death the sinful deeds of the body (8:13). Grace supplies to the regenerate the strength to resist the world, Satan, and the flesh and the power to gain the victory over them (Eph 6:11-18; Jas 4:4-8, 1 John 4:4, 5:4). Arminius objected that this modern opinion attributes to grace in the regenerate only the power to *will* and not to *do*. It is too weak to crucify the old man, to destroy the body of sin, or to conquer the flesh, the world, and Satan. Can the contest described in this chapter be ascribed to the indwelling Holy Spirit without bringing dishonor to the grace of Christ and of his Spirit? Is not the Holy Spirit represented as being much weaker than indwelling sin?

A regenerate man fights in the power and strength of the grace and the Spirit of Christ. Therefore, if while fighting he is conquered, the grace and the Spirit of Christ are overcome;

---

[187]*Lange's Commentary*, 5:245.

this would be most dishonoring to the grace and Spirit of Christ. If he is conquered while in a state of nonresistance after he has cast away his weapons or has ceased from the combat, that is another matter. The circumstances Paul states is a man who is made prisoner while in actual combat. If this describes a regenerate man, nothing could be more harmful to good morals. Those who adopt this position can then flatter themselves that they are regenerate, while sinning, simply because they sinned with a reluctant conscience and with a will that offered some resistance.

Therefore, such an interpretation is injurious to grace, because it lays down as a sign of regeneration that which is common to both the regenerate and the unregenerate who are under the condemnation of the law. It is also contrary to good morals because the man who holds such opinions does not strive as hard to avoid sin nor does the commitment of sin produce deep sorrow in him since he concludes that he is still regenerate.

The regenerate may sin; but, when they sin they do so willingly. Arminius argued that they do not proceed onward to the act of sin until the battle between the mind and the flesh is over and the will has consented to the flesh. Such an agreement cannot be made without a stinging remorse of conscience. It is not likely that sin should obtain a full consent from the will of that man who is generally well instructed in the righteousness and unrighteousness of action, unless he has ceased to feel any sorrow or regret. For the conscience continues even after the Holy Spirit has either departed completely or has been so grieved that he does not continue to work.[188] All of the associates and successors of Arminius, such as Hugo Grotius, Simon Episcopius, and Philip Limborch,

---

[188]This concludes a summary of Arminius [*Works*, 2:488-683].

adopted the same view.

John Wesley said Paul is writing of a person under the law. He assumes another character to show the weakness and inefficiency of the law. "To have spoken this of himself, or any true believer, would have been foreign to the whole scope of his discourse, nay, utterly contrary thereto."[189] In response to Dr. John Taylor, Wesley wrote, "And this whole chapter, from the 7th to 24th verse, describes the state of all those, Jews or Gentiles, who *saw* and *felt* the wickedness both of their hearts and lives, and groaned to be delivered from it."[190]

John Fletcher said that Paul describes in his own person the uncomfortable state of the carnal penitent in Romans 7.[191] In his *Last Check to Antinomianism*, Fletcher devoted an entire section to Romans 7. He challenged the Calvinists of his day to drop "the yoke of carnality which they try to fix upon St. Paul's neck." Fletcher declared that Paul no more professes himself actually a carnal man than he professes himself actually a liar in Romans 3:7. Fletcher thought it was not worse to represent the apostle as a church robber than to libel him as "a wretched, carnal man, sold under sin." Fletcher observed that the opening verses of Romans 7 described the liberty of a spiritual man:

> We have, therefore, in Romans 7:4-6, a strong rampart against the mistake which our opponents build on the rest of the chapter. This mistake will appear still more astonishing, if we read Romans 6, where

---

[189]Wesley, *Notes*, 379. See also "The Spirit of Bondage and Adoption," 2.9

[190]Wesley, *BE Works*, 12:283.

[191]Fletcher, *Works*, 1:542.

the apostle particularly describes the liberty of those who "serve God in newness of the spirit," according to the glorious privileges of the new covenant. . . . We shall see their mistake in a still more glaring light if we pass to Romans 8, and consider the description which St. Paul continues to give us of the glorious liberty of those who have done with "the oldness of the [Jewish] letter, and serve God in newness of the Spirit.

Fletcher concluded that Romans 7:7-25, "show how the *unawakened* sinner is roused out of his carnal state, and how the *awakened* sinner is driven to Christ for liberty by the lashing and binding commandment."[192]

Richard Watson wrote that whether Paul

speaks of himself or describes the state of others in a supposed case, given for the sake of more vivid representation in the first person, which is more probable, he is clearly speaking of a person who had once sought justification by the works of the law, but who was then convinced, by the force of a spiritual apprehension of the extent of the requirements of that law, and by constant failures in his attempts to keep it perfectly, that he was in bondage to his corrupt nature, and could only be delivered from this thraldom by the interposition of another. For, not to urge that his strong expressions of being "carnal," "sold under sin," and doing always "the things which he would not," are utterly inconsistent with that moral state of believers in Christ which he de-

---

[192]Fletcher, *Works*, 2:529-540.

scribes in the next chapter.[193]

In *Conversations for the Young*, Watson wrote that Paul may speak of his own experience when under the law, but not of his experience as a believer, because in 8:2 he is free from the law, or power, of sin and death. It is rather to be considered that in both chapters Paul speaks general truths in his own person, "a common mode with all writers."[194]

Adam Clarke wrote that although Paul uses the personal pronoun *I*,

> he cannot mean *himself,* nor any *Christian believer*: If the contrary could be proved, the argument of the apostle would go to demonstrate the insufficiency of the *Gospel,* as well as the *law.* It is difficult to conceive how the opinion could have crept into the Church, or prevailed there, that "the apostle speaks here of his *regenerate state.*" ... This opinion has most pitifully and most shamefully, not only lowered the standard of Christianity, but destroyed its influence and disgraced its character. . . . From all this it follows that the epithet *carnal,* which is the characteristic designation of an unregenerate man, cannot be applied to St. Paul, *after his conversion;* nor, indeed, to any *Christian* in that state."[195]

Thomas Coke said, "There are few chapters in sacred Scripture which have been more misrepresented or misunder-

---

[193]Watson, *Theological Institutes*, 2:451.

[194]Watson, *Conversations for the Young*, 343-344.

[195]Clarke, *Commentary*, 6:86.

stood, than that before us." Paul "cannot be supposed . . . to describe the state of a Christian, unless he can be supposed to represent the Gospel as weak and defective as the law itself. . . . To hear some persons talk, one would imagine that they thought it their duty, and a mark of sincerity and goodness, to be always complaining of corrupt and desperately wicked hearts." But Coke declared this was a "false humility." "Whoever carefully peruses the New Testament will find, that however we are obligated to repent of sin, a spirit of *complaining and bewailing* is not the spirit of the Gospel; neither is it the rule of true religion, nor any mark of sincerity, to have a corrupt heart, or to be always complaining of such a heart. On the contrary, the gospel is intended to deliver us from all iniquity, and to purify us into a peculiar people zealous of good works, and to sanctify us throughout in body, soul, and spirit, that we may *now* be saints, — may *now* have peace and joy in the Holy Ghost, and at length be presented without spot or blemish, before the presence of God."

Coke taught that this chapter describes the awakened, but yet unregenerate. Paul describes "the struggle between reason and passion, which arises in the mind of the sinner when awakened through the Divine Spirit by the operation of law on his conscience."[196]

Joseph Sutcliffe wrote, "What a pity then that any commentator should wish to apply this lamentable portrait to St. Paul at the time he wrote, for it makes him contradict himself. . . . Oh, sinner, how long wilt thou remain in this most degrading servitude, seeing Christ is come to make thee free."[197] Joseph Benson wrote:

---

[196]Coke, *Commentary*, 6:72, 78-79.

[197]Sutcliffe, *Commentary*, 2:457-458.

Those commentators, therefore, who suppose that in this and what follows, to the end of the chapter, the apostle describes his own state, at the time he wrote this epistle, and consequently the state of every regenerated person, must be under a great mistake. Universally, indeed, in the Scriptures, man is said to be in this state of bondage to sin until the Son of God make him free; but in no part of the sacred writings is it ever said of the children of God, that they are *sold under sin,* or enslaved to it. The very reverse is the Holy Spirit's description of Christians, for *the Son* of God *makes them free,* and therefore *they are free indeed;* free especially from the power of sin, which has no longer domination over them.[198]

George Peck declared, "Now I affirm, on the contrary, that the language of the seventh chapter of Romans does not accord 'with the experience of Christians.'" In the context Peck was refuting the inconsistencies of Charles Hodge. Peck observed that such commentators are compelled to give a sense to the language of Paul in chapters 6 and 8 which cannot be made to harmonize with what is found in the seventh chapter. Peck then refuted the arguments of Daniel Whitby by utilizing the writings of Arminius.[199]

Daniel Whedon felt that Romans 7:7-25 was a parenthesis in Paul's train of thought. This is the narrative of an unregenerate man, under the law and in the flesh. Whedon also wrote that for the first three centuries the entire Christian church with one accord applied this passage solely to the

---

[198]Benson, *Notes,* 5:62.

[199]Peck, *Christian Perfection,* 295-321, 394.

unregenerate man. "Its application to the regenerate man was first invented by Augustine, who was followed by many eminent doctors of the Middle Ages. After the Reformation the interpretation by Augustine was largely adopted, especially by the followers of Calvin."

Whedon noted in his commentary that Charles Hodge expressed the opinion that Romans 7 was the ordinary language of Christian experience. Whedon replied, "It is so only . . . in accordance with and in consequence of a theological teaching that requires it. No such language, either doctrinal or practical, is found in the Christian writings of the first three centuries."[200]

Thomas Summers asked if this was Paul's own experience as a Christian, freed from sin and from the law. Surely Paul never meant to express a dualism in which he could possess two natures and serve two masters. Summers associated this interpretation with Manicheism, an ancient dualistic philosophy which was essentially gnostic. Summers also declared that until Augustine changed his position, no one held such an interpretation. He suggested that all who hold such a view have never read the masterly dissertation by Arminius.[201]

J. Agar Beet held that Paul was describing his own experience before justification. "We have here the fullest description in the Bible of man unsaved. . . . If the words before us refer to a justified man, they stand absolutely alone in the entire New Testament."[202]

Amos Binney wrote that for the first three hundred years

---

[200]Whedon, *Commentary*, 3:335-337.

[201]Summers, *Commentary*, 82-93.

[202]Beet, *Commentary*, 206-210.

the Christian church, with one accord, applied this passage to the *unregenerate* man. Augustine abandoned his former position in defense of his views on predestination and applied this passage to the *regenerate* man. "The correct interpretation lies, probably, between the two extreme views. The passage evidently describes the *natural* man, yet not the man *without law*, as in verses 5, 8, 9; but the *awakened sinner* under the law, in the transition period in which he is led of the Spirit from the law to Christ." Thus, the conflict described in Romans 7 is the "warfare between *indwelling sin* and *conscience* in awakened and convicted sinner."[203]

Daniel Steele gave five objections to the interpretation that this chapter is the portrait of the regenerate soul:

- Such a life must be under continual condemnation, which is inconsistent with justification.
- Such exegesis makes the gospel as great a failure as the law in its reconstruction of human character.
- Such an interpretation makes Paul contradict what he teaches in Romans 6 and 8. Nowhere else does Paul intimate that sin dwells in him. How could a man living in Romans 7 exhort, "Be ye imitators of me, even as I also am of Christ" (1 Cor 11:1)?
- Are we to understand that carnality is the dominant principle in the regenerate? In Romans 7:7-24 there is no term which implies the new birth or spirituality. In the whole contest the Spirit does not appear on the field as one of the combatants. The two parties to the contest are reason and passion. This is entirely different from the strife of the Spirit against the flesh in Galatians 5:17.
- The Greek fathers, during the first three hundred years of

---

[203]Binney, *The People's Commentary*, 410-411.

church history, unanimously interpreted this Scripture as describing a thoughtful moralist endeavoring without the grace of God to realize his highest ideal of moral purity. Augustine at first followed this interpretation, until his debate with Pelagius. Pelegius used vv 14 and 22 to prove that the natural man can appreciate the beauty of holiness and therefore was not depraved. To cut Pelegius off from this argument, Augustine adopted a new theory that this chapter is a description of the regenerate.[204]

More recently Wilbur Dayton wrote, "Paul is looking back on the plight from the position of a born-again person. This was his plight under the law — in sin. This would still be his plight and ours but for redemption."[205]

Kenneth Grider explained that vv 12 and 22 do not describe a regenerate person, but should be interpreted in light of prevenient grace. Grider upheld the view of Arminius that the inner man in v 22 is not regenerate. Grider also pointed out that both the unregenerate and the regenerate have a sinful nature. The fact that vv 17 and 20 refer to indwelling sin, therefore, does not prove the subject is regenerate. Grider also argued in light of the hermeneutical principle that we should not interpret a writer in such a way that he contradicts himself in the same document and that Romans 7 cannot be made to contradict Romans 8. Therefore, Romans 7, although it uses the present tense, is Paul's lively way of describing his earlier experience.[206]

---

[204]Steele, *Half-Hours with St. Paul*, 70-76; Oden, *Life in the Spirit*, 245-246.

[205]Dayton, *Wesleyan Bible Commentary*, 5:51.

[206]Grider, *Entire Sanctification*, 141-143.

Thus, in a span of over three hundred fifty years, we have surveyed the interpretation of Arminius and the early Remonstrants, as well as every classic Methodist theologian and commentator. While there is some variance over whether Paul is describing his personal state or speaking in general, there is a remarkable unity that the person Paul describes is not regenerate. Added to this united voice is the fact that the early church, for its first three hundred years, also held the same position.

5. The Holiness Interpretation

The holiness movement claims to be Wesleyan in doctrine; but like Augustine who changed his interpretation of Romans 7 in the heat of controversy, the holiness movement adopted a Calvinistic interpretation of Romans 7 in an attempt to demonstrate the necessity of a second blessing.

Kenneth Grider claims the teaching among the holiness movement that Romans 7 depicts a regenerate person is only occasional and that it is "folk theology," but the holiness movement perpetuated a lot more folk theology than Grider acknowledged.[207] W. B. Godbey commented:

> While this seventh chapter is the personal experience of Paul and all other sanctified Christians, we do not reach the epoch of his receiving the blessing till verse 25, the preceding chapter constituting his testimony to the battle with inbred sin.... While you read this chapter you will understand it better if you keep your eye on Paul down in Arabia, wallowing in the burning sands and fighting inbred sin like a dog

---

[207] Grider, *Entire Sanctification*, 141-142.

in a yellow-jackets' nest.[208]

Every Christian, when converted, sets out to obey the Lord on earth like the angels in heaven, thus keeping the law in the beauty of holiness; but destined to defeat, failure, mortification despondency, culminating in desperation, like Paul in the verse when he cried out, "O wretched man that I am!"[209]

Beverly Carradine wrote that this chapter cannot be confined to a Jew under the law nor any legalist. The man in this chapter is not spiritually dead by any means. Carradine adopts the Calvinistic interpretation, pointing to v 22 as evidence of regeneration. Still further proof of the regenerated state of this man is found in v 25. "He that consents to — serves and delights in — the law of God is a saved man!" declared Carradine. He called for the reader to divest himself of prejudice. "The Church might as well come to it. The battle has already started on this chapter, and we see nothing but victory for the cause of holiness in what will transpire in the probing study and honest application of this chapter." Ironically, "for the cause of holiness," Carradine devoted an entire chapter to undermining the historic Wesleyan interpretation of Romans 7.[210]

Henry Clay Morrison wrote:

> The Christian reader will at once recognize the undoubted truthfulness of these Scriptures for they are corroborated by the every-day experience of believ-

---

[208]Godbey, *Commentary*, 5:104.

[209]Godbey, *Commentary*, 5:117.

[210]Carradine, *The Old Man*, 93-111.

ing souls, who, struggling against the "old man," have often been made to cry out, "O wretched man that I am, who shall deliver me from the body of this death? The baptism with the Holy Ghost casts out the "old man." ... This is entire sanctification.[211]

Grider wrote that Morrison

did not seem to know that James Arminius wrote over 250 pages on that chapter, taking an "awakened unregenerate" view of the person there described — and starting a long and stable and almost unanimous tradition of such interpretation in Arminian-Wesleyanism.[212]

Charles E. Brown wrote, "Assuming, then, that we have in this chapter an account of the experience of a true and even of an advanced Christian, we learn that in every Christian there is a mixture of good and evil."[213] These statements agree more with Calvinism than with early Methodism.

In *Great Holiness Classics: Holiness Teaching Today*, not only are the statements by Morrison and Brown reprinted, but Milton Agnew describes Christian experience:

After conversion he discovers in himself a new nature that does "joyfully concur with the law of God" (Romans 7:22). But he learns to his distress that he

---

[211] Morrison, *Baptism with the Holy Ghost*, 24. This booklet was reprinted in *Great Holiness Classics*, 6:24-47.

[212] Grider, *A Wesleyan-Holiness Theology*, 464.

[213] Brown, *The Meaning of Sanctification*, 27, 25, 29, 64.

also has an old nature, an "old self," aroused and battling for supremacy. There occurs a profoundly disturbing struggle between the two natures, the two "I's" of 7:14-25.[214]

In *More Than Conquerors*, Agnew wrote that Romans 7 describes a regenerate man seeking deliverance in his own strength from the power of sin.[215]

After A. M. Hills quoted Fletcher saying that Romans 7 was an awakened sinner, Hills concluded, "Whether Paul in this famous passage was picturing a carnal sinner or a carnal Christian, he was certainly not picturing his own best experience nor the best possible experience of any Christian."[216]

George McLaughlin wrote that Paul was describing the struggle against inbred sin, whether in the unregenerate or the regenerate. "We say it can be shown to be the experience of both."[217]

A. Skevington Wood believed that Romans 6-8 dealt with sanctification and that 7:7-25 was autobiographical. While he acknowledged that is could refer to Paul's Damascus Road experience, he argued that it was more likely referring to his sojourn in Arabia described in Galatians 1:17, which came *after* Paul's conversion.[218]

Even though Henry Brockett stated clearly that Romans

---

[214]Agnew, *More Than Conquerors*, cited in *Holiness Teaching Today*, Harper, ed., 146.

[215]Agnew, *More Than Conquerors*, 93-96.

[216]Hills, *Fundamental Christian Theology*, 2:259.

[217]McLaughlin, *Commentary,* 126.

[218]Wood, *Life by the Spirit*, 22.

7 was not Christian experience, he tended to muddy this statement by his interpretation that Romans 6 and 8 are dealing with sanctification and "the full blessing of Pentecost," which he associated with a second work of grace. Therefore, Brockett concluded that the experience of bondage described is not of a regenerate man, but the climax of his self-discovery *after* his regeneration. He concluded that the bondage, defeat, and humiliation experienced by the Christian are *analogous* to the bondage portrayed in Romans 7.[219]

While claiming to follow John Wesley, their apologetic for a second blessing is based more on the two-natures theology of Lewis Chafer. For example, *The Old Man* is not about the sinner who needs to get saved, but about the Christian with two natures. Elmer G. Marsh wrote:

> It is a sad fact according to experience that many regenerated saints do not always suppress the old man. They, at times, give way to his stirrings and must repent and ask God's forgiveness. Thus man lives an up and down life for a time.[220]

While Marsh and Chafer would disagree over eternal security and eradication language, this believer described by Marsh as "up and down" sounds identical to the Christian on Walvoord's "spiritual seesaw." John Wesley said that the justified are "so far perfect, as not to commit sin."[221] However, the holiness movement of the 19th century began to

---

[219]Brockett, *The Christian and Romans 7*, 85, 109-110, 157.

[220]Marsh, *The Old Man*, 63. Marsh was president of God's Bible School 1961-1965.

[221]Wesley, "Christian Perfection," Sermon #40, 2.20-21.

teach that one who was born again was still carnal and needed to move to a higher state — the Spirit-filled life.

While the second work of grace is promised as a cure-all to rectify the deficiencies of the new birth, in actuality, it is often obtained by the "name it and claim it" method; and the seeker who professes it at some point faces the realization that he is haunted by the same old sins. The modern holiness movement is as powerless as the rest of the nominal church and is not exempt from the antinomianism that plagues every other denomination.

> One consequence of this has been the coming of an instruction, the type of which noticeably cheapens the concept of the first work of God in the heart so as to make room, so to speak, for the second. The end product is distressing, for we find those who have been professing believers for some time, who later experience for the *first time* the kingdom of heaven within and conclude they are entirely sanctified. Others there are who in a similar fashion lightly pass over the first work, seek and claim the second and attain neither. Some who seek the second experience attain only to a reclamation of the first, but claim both, etc. We therefore believe it to be very urgent that a renewed emphasis upon and understanding of the first work be revived in the present day Church.[222]

Henry Williams rejected the idea that

> the Apostle here delineates the experience of *a re-*

---

[222]McPherson, "What Manner of Man Is He?" 6-8.

generate man, but one *not yet confirmed in holiness.* For this would be in direct opposition to the view which he gives of the position and state of *all* who are in Christ Jesus, but in the chapter preceding this, and in that which immediately follows.[223]

6. Recent Developments

John Knox ignored the historic Wesleyan-Arminian interpretation when he wrote the exegesis for *The Interpreter's Bible* in 1954. "There is nothing in Paul's *language* to suggest that he is remembering the past rather than describing the present. . . . He is simply reporting what he finds true of himself in the very moment of writing. . . . We shall assume that Paul in this passage is not merely remembering an earlier situation, but is also speaking naturally and sincerely out of his present experience."[224]

Contemporary Wesleyan writers, such as Joseph Wang, conclude that Romans 7 describes non-Christians and Christians who have not experienced "the second work of grace."[225] This lowers regeneration and lumps together the struggles of saved and unsaved. Writing in *The Wesley Bible*, Wang notes, "Non-Christians who have been convicted by the Holy Spirit live with this struggle. Also Christians who are not living a victorious life in the Spirit experience similar struggle, even though God has given them a measure of victory over sin."[226]

---

[223]Henry Williams, *Exposition*, 198.

[224]*The Interpreter's Bible*, 9:499-500, published by Abingdon-Cokesbury Press of the Methodist Church.

[225]Wang, *Asbury Bible Commentary*, 988-989.

[226]Harper, ed. *The Wesley Bible*, 1692.

Although Greathouse interpreted vv 14-25 as having a primary application to the unrenewed man, yet he interjects a degree of confusion by allowing a secondary application for the Christian. Greathouse wrote, "Something of this divided condition and occasional defeat is therefore present experience for the believer until he is cleansed from remaining sin by the sanctifying power of the Spirit."[227] Richard S. Taylor also wanted Romans 7 to describe both the unregenerate and the unsanctified.[228]

However, in the *New Beacon Bible Commentary*, written forty years later, Greathouse challenged the 19th century holiness interpretation which understood Romans 7 as a description of the justified but unsanctified believer. "This 'I' hardly seems a fit candidate for entire sanctification." Greathouse concluded:

> Clearly the conflicted "I," the "wretched" person in Rom 7 is an awakened sinner, struggling for deliverance from indwelling sin. To apply these versed to the normal Christian believer would be to admit that the grace of Christ is as powerless against sin as the law of Moses![229]

Richard E. Howard wrote, "How can such *total* spiritual wretchedness be reconciled with the saving grace of God?

---

[227]Greathouse, *Beacon Bible Commentary*, 8:160; see also Purkiser, *Exploring Christian Holiness*, 1:112-144. McCant highlighted the contradictions in Greathouse's treatment of Romans 7 ["The Wesleyan Interpretation of Romans 5-8," 43].

[228]Taylor, *Life in the Spirit*, 50.

[229]Greathouse, *Romans 1-8*, 222-223.

Instead this graphic picture is most likely how Paul views the life he once lived under the law — but *now* seen through the eyes of his new life in Christ." Then Howard surrenders his Wesleyan position in a footnote: "If this is a picture of a Christian, then he is a defeated Christian, and this defeat is the result of trying to live *kata sarka* [according to the flesh]."[230]

The *Reflecting God Study Bible*, based upon *The NIV Study Bible*, which had a more Calvinistic bias, retained the note by Walter Wessel that the phrase "sold as a slave to sin" is "so strong that many refuse to accept it as descriptive of a Christian." Yet Roger Green, the "Wesleyan" writer added, "However, it may graphically point out the failure even of Christians to meet the radical ethical and moral requirements of the gospel, and to live the life that holiness demands." He concludes, "However ch. 7 is interpreted, ch. 8 triumphantly announces life in the Spirit available for every Christian."[231]

The third "Wesleyan" study Bible, *The Wesley Study Bible*, cited Wesley, "To have spoken this of himself, or any true believer, would have been foreign to the whole scope of his discourse." Two sentences later we are told, "Paul describes a state to which believers may revert, not one in which he expects them to remain."[232]

It creates confusion when Wesleyan-Arminian "authorities" fail to maintain this fundamental position of the Wesleyan-Arminian tradition. Our apologetic for entire sanctification should never be the failure of regeneration. Ironically, while some holiness writers have muddied the position

---

[230]Howard, *Newness of Life*, 51-52.

[231]McCown, *The Reflecting God Study Bible*, 1718.

[232]Green and Willimon, eds. *The Wesley Study Bible*, 1376.

of Arminius, some Calvinists have moved closer to Arminius. Herman N. Ridderbos, in his 1959 Dutch commentary on Romans, defended the view that 7:14-25 portrays a man apart from Christ who is engaged in a desperate struggle under the law. Ridderbos argued that if the *I* described in v 14 indicates a person redeemed by Christ and led by the Spirit, how is this man superior to the power of sin in v 13? The *now* of 8:1 does not represent the deplorable situation of 7:14-25, but a situation which arises afterward. The reign of the Spirit cannot be identified with, but follows, the reign of sin. According to 6:2, 6, 7, 11, 12, 13, 17, 18, 22 sin is the dethroned lord for the Christian. Sin has lost its ruling power. In fact, all of chapter 6 is a continuous refutation of the position that the *I* of 7:14-25 could represent the new man redeemed by Christ.[233]

Anthony A. Hoekema, Professor Emeritus of Systematic Theology at Calvin Theological Seminary, wrote in 1987, "I now see this passage as a description, seen through the eyes of a regenerate person, of an unregenerate person.... I admit that this position is not the usual Reformed interpretation." Hoekema then proceeds to give four reasons for his view:

- Romans 7:14-25 reflects and elaborates on the condition pictured in vv 5 and 13, obviously an unregenerate person.
- There is no mention of the Holy Spirit in vv 14-25, but

---

[233]Ridderbos is summarized by Hendriksen, *Commentary*, 225-226. Hendriksen attempted to rebut each of the three points made by Ridderbos, but Ridderbos is more convincing. Hendriksen wrote that W. G. Kümmel's 1929 book on Romans 7 has been responsible, perhaps more than any other 20th century work, to perpetuate the interpretation that Paul was describing an unbeliever.

he is mentioned at least sixteen times in chapter 8.

- "The mood of frustration and defeat that permeates this section does not comport with the mood of victory in terms of which Paul usually describes the Christian life."
- The words "I myself" in v 25 are emphatic in Greek. Paul is here describing a person who tries to "go it alone," rather than with the help of the Spirit.[234]

While Lloyd-Jones usually champions the Calvinistic position, he wrestled to identify the spiritual state of the person described in this chapter for some eighty pages. He declared repeatedly that this was not the description of either an unregenerate or a regenerate person. He finally concluded that this person is under deep conviction of sin.[235] Thus, the person is awakened, but not yet regenerate. Thus, the description is of conviction but not conversion. Methodist commentators have consistently taken the same position. Sometimes the Methodist position is categorized as teaching the man of Romans 7 is unsaved. Other positions which are frequently listed include carnal Christian, convicted or mature Christian. However, the categories of unsaved and convicted are not contradictory. While a sinner could be either awakened or unawakened, the awakened person is still unsaved.

Thomas R. Schreiner, who has written in defense of

---

[234]Hoekema, "Response to Walvoord," 232, 243. This is a retraction of Hoekema's "The Struggle Between the Old and New Natures in the Converted Man," 42-50.

[235]Lloyd-Jones, *The Law*, 176-257; summary statement , p. 256. However, he is not entirely consistent. For strong statements that the man is unregenerate, see pp. 192, 194, 209, 239-243, 247-248, 251, 254, 256-257. For strong statements that the man is regenerate, see pp. 192, 198-199, 217-218, 224.

Calvinistic positions, also seemed reluctant to conclude that this chapter describes the whole of Christian experience. While Schreiner said that complete deliverance from sin is not available for Christians until the day of redemption, the hope of future deliverance should not exclude present victory. We should not conclude that believers are utterly helpless under the power of sin.[236]

R. J. Rushdoony wrote that v 15 describes the dominion of sin over the sinner. But the promise of 6:14, that sin shall not have dominion over us, is the promise to the regenerate. Rushdoony has also backed away from the dogmatism that consent (v 22) must describe the regenerate.[237]

Douglas Moo stated the purpose of his 1991 commentary on Romans was to reassert the Reformers' theology in light of current scholarship and contemporary challenges. After stating the leading arguments for both major interpretations of Romans 7, Moo concluded that vv 14-25 "describe the situation of an unregenerate person." Moo said that two sets of contrasts tipped the scales in favor of this view.

First, the description of the *ego* as "sold under sin" (v 14b) and Paul's assertion that every believer has been set free from sin (6:18, 22).

Second, the contrast between the *ego* "imprisoned by the law (or power) of sin" (v 23) and the believer who has been "set free from the law of sin and death" (8:2).

Moo stated, "Each of these expressions depicts an objective status, and it is difficult to see how they can all be applied to the same person in the same spiritual condition without

---

[236] Schreiner, *Commentary*, 390-391.

[237] Rushdoony, *Systematic Theology*, 1:487-489.

doing violence to Paul's language."²³⁸

Sinclair Ferguson, professor of systematic theology at Westminster Theological Seminary, wrote that since the 1929 publication of W. G. Kümmel's monograph, *Romans 7 and the Conversion of Paul*, interpretation has continued to shift away from the view that Romans 7 describes Paul's Christian life. Ferguson admits that expressions such as "sold as a slave under sin," a "prisoner of the law of sin," "a wretched man," and "a slave to the law of sin" are difficult to reconcile with Paul's descriptions of life in the Spirit. Ultimately, Ferguson clings to his Calvinistic tradition but concludes that his view should not be taken to suggest that Paul views the Christian as paralyzed by sin and the flesh. Rather, it is the Christian's task to put to death the misdeeds of the body.²³⁹

In 2008 Dennis Johnson wrote "The Function of Romans 7:13-25 in Paul's Argument for the Law's Impotence and the Spirit's Power, and It's Bearing on the Schizophrenic 'I.'" In this chapter Johnson takes the position that this describes pre-conversion.²⁴⁰ Robert Reymond also departs from Augustine in "Whom Does the Man in Romans 7:14-25 Represent?"²⁴¹

In addition to these recent Calvinistic scholars who have shifted over the last generation or two, David C. Needham, writing as a dispensationalist, also concluded, "I believe that it is completely illogical to hold that Romans 7:14-25 is describing the typical experience of a believer who is looking at

---

²³⁸Moo, *Romans 1-8*, 474-475. Moo makes the same statements in his *NICNT*, 447-449.

²³⁹Ferguson, *The Holy Spirit*, 156-162.

²⁴⁰Johnson, *Resurrection and Eschatology*, 3-59.

²⁴¹Reymond, *A New Systematic Theology*, 1127-1132.

life through the truth of Romans 6 and 8."[242]

Pentecostal scholar Gordon Fee wrote that Paul was describing his life before and outside Christ. Fee observed that Paul is describing life under the law, not life in Christ. Paul does not so much as mention the Spirit. Fee saw 7:7-25 as a digression; 8:5-8 describe life before and after Christ. Fee also thought it is significant that in 8:12-13, when Paul offers his warning, he shifts from *we* to *you*, signifying that Paul does not consider those who live after the flesh as Christians.[243]

Our attempt to understand this chapter is influenced by our own experience. Alexander Whyte, often described as "the last of the Puritans," told his congregation, "You'll never get out of the seventh of Romans while I'm your minister." He meant that he would constantly remind them that they were, at best, sinners.[244]

Karl Barth, who also believed Paul was describing his own present experience and discounted the interpretation of "those modern theologians who read him through the specta-

---

[242]Needham, *Birthright*, 65. Walvoord attempts to dismiss this traitor within the ranks by claiming Needham denies there is a sin nature in believers ["The Augustinian-Dispensational Perspective," 207]. This misses the point entirely. The issue is whether Christians are so bound by sin that they even sin involuntarily.

[243]Fee, *God's Empowering Presence*, 511-515. In *Romans and the People of God*, written in honor of Gordon Fee, J. I. Packer revisited Rom 7:14-25, restated his same arguments, did not interact with Fee's observations, and then concluded that, with due respect to his honored colleague, he remains a convinced and unrepentant Augustinian with regard to the "wretched man" ["The 'Wretched Man' Revisited," 70-81].

[244]Packer, *Keep in Step with the Spirit*, 129.

cles of their own piety. . . . He portrays a situation as real after the episode on the road to Damascus as before it."[245] In 2021, Christiane Tietz's *Karl Barth: A Life in Conflict* was published in English for the first time. Although the true nature of Karl Barth's relationship with his secretary, assistant, and "co-labourer" Charlotte von Kirschbaum had been public for some time, Tietz's book recounts this decades-long extramarital relationship. Was his theology based upon his own justification of this adultery? Should not our personal experience be judged in light of God's Word instead of God's Word interpreted in light of our personal experience?

The church must be "always reforming" and it is refreshing to see honest scholars reexamine traditional positions in light of Scripture. We need to return back to the historic position of the church. If our understanding of salvation is not based upon our own subjective experience, but upon the teaching in Romans which has preceded and which follows this section, then we are left with no choice but to conclude, along with the unanimous opinion of all the classic Wesleyan-Arminian writers, that this section does not describe the freedom from sin that is consistent with the new birth.

But theology should be based on Scriptural exegesis, not on personal experience, theological presuppositions, or philosophy. Wesley advised, "Try all things by the written Word, and let all bow down before it."[246] Albert Outler, in his annotation to Wesley's sermons, got it backwards when he wrote, "Obviously, one's exegesis here follows from one's soteriology and not from any decisive evidence within the

---

[245]Barth, *Epistle to the Romans*, 270.

[246]Wesley, *BE Works*, 13:113.

Greek text."[247]

The rebirth of patristics studies is largely the result of Thomas Oden's influence. Yet we must go beyond the early church fathers. Authority is vested in the biblical text. The church fathers believed the Scriptures. Thus, they reflect, to a large degree, biblical teaching.

While Arminius was part of the Reformation, he took a minority Reformation position based on Scriptural exegesis. Today that same position is becoming a minority position within Calvinism. My friends within the conservative holiness movement also assure me that there is a growing acceptance that Romans 7 describes pre-conversion.

Ultimately this debate is not about defending theological positions. Rather, it is over what Scripture teaches. The evangelical antinomianism of the 20th century demonstrated the result of a misunderstanding of Romans 7. The highest state of Christian life is described in 1 Corinthians 13, not Romans 7. Hopefully, honest Scriptural exegesis will cause the reexamination of theological presuppositions which will lead to pastoral teaching that does not advocate "miserable Christianity," but deliverance from the guilt, the power, and the bondage of sin.

---

[247]Wesley, *BE Works*, 1:260.

Bibliography

Adams, Gwenfair Walters. *Reformation Commentary on Scripture: Romans 1-8*. Vol. 7. Timothy George, ed. Downers Grove, IL: InterVarsity, 2019.

Agnew, Milton S. *More Than Conquerors*. 1977. Cited in *Holiness Teaching Today*. Vol. 6 of *Great Holiness Classics*. Albert F. Harper, ed. Kansas City: Beacon Hill, 1987.

Ambrose. *Letters. Nicene and Post Nicene Fathers*. Philip Schaff and Henry Wace, eds. Second Series. Volume 10. 1888. Reprint, Grand Rapids: Eerdmans, 1979.

Ambrosiaster. *Ancient Christian Texts: Commentaries on Galatians – Philemon*. Gerald L. Bray, ed. Downers Grove, IL: InterVarsity, 2009. [ACT]

Arminius, James. *The Works of James Arminius: The London Edition*. 3 vols. transl by James and William Nichols. 1828; Reprint, Grand Rapids: Baker, 1996.

Augustine, Aurelius. *Against Two Letters of the Pelagians. The Nicene and Post-Nicene Fathers*. Philip Schaff, ed. First Series. Volume 5. 1887. Reprint, Grand Rapids: Eerdmans, 1971.

Ayars, Matt, Christopher T. Bounds, and Caleb T. Friedeman. *Holiness: A Biblical, Historical, and Systematic Theology*. Downers Grove, IL: InterVarsity, 2023.

Bahnsen, Greg L. *By This Standard*. Tyler, TX: Institute for Christian Economics, 1985.

Bangs, Carl. *Arminius, A Study in the Dutch Reformation*. 1971.

Reprint, Grand Rapids: Francis Asbury Press, 1985.

Barnhouse, Donald Grey. *Expositions of Bible Doctrines Taking the Epistle to the Romans as a Point of Departure*. 10 vols. Grand Rapids: Eerdmans, 1952-1964.

Barth, Karl. *Epistle to the Romans*. 6th ed. Edwyn C. Hiskyns, transl. London: Oxford University Press, 1933.

Barrett, C. K. *A Commentary on the Epistle to the Romans*. New York: Harper & Row, 1957. Rev. ed. *Black's New Testament Commentary*. London: Continuum, 1991.

Basil. *Concerning Baptism*. Vol. 9 *The Fathers of the Church: Saint Basil Ascetical Works*. M. Monica Wagner, transl. New York: Fathers of the Church, 1950.

Beet, Joseph Agar. *A Commentary on St. Paul's Epistle to the Romans*. 10th ed. 1902. Reprint, Salem, OH: Allegheny, 1982.

Benson, Joseph. *The Holy Bible, with Notes, All the Marginal Readings, Summaries, and the Date of Every Transaction*. 2nd ed. 5 vols. 1811-1815. Reprint, New York: Carlton & Phillips, 1856.

Binney, Amos and Daniel Steele. *The People's Commentary on the New Testament*. New York: Eaton & Mains, 1878.

Blackwelder, Boyce W. *Toward Understanding Romans*. Anderson, IN: Warner, 1962.

_____. Light from the Greek New Testament. 1958. Reprint, Grand Rapids: Baker, 1976.

Boice, James Montgomery. *Romans*. 4 vols. Grand Rapids: Baker, 1991-1995

Bonnet, Louis. *Épitres de Paul*. 1875; quoted by Frederick Godet. *Commentary on the Epistle to the Romans*. 1883; Reprint, Grand Rapids: Zondervan, 1956.

Bray, Gerald, ed. *Ancient Christian Commentary on Scripture*. Thomas C. Oden, gen. ed. *Romans*. Vol. 6. Downers Grove, IL: InterVarsity, 1998. [*ACCS*]

Brockett, Henry E. *The Christian and Romans 7*. Kansas City: Beacon Hill, 1972.

Brown, Charles Ewing. *The Meaning of Sanctification*. 1945. Reprint, Salem, OH: Schmul, 1980.

Bruce, F. F. *Tyndale New Testament Commentaries: Romans*. Grand Rapids: Eerdmans, 1963.

Burwash, Nathaniel, ed. *Wesley's Doctrinal Standards*. Toronto: William Briggs, 1881.

_____. *A Handbook of the Epistle of St. Paul to the Romans*. 2nd ed. Toronto: William Briggs, 1900.

Calvin, John. *Commentaries on the Epistle of Paul the Apostle to the Romans*. John Owen, transl. and ed. Grand Rapids: Eerdmans, 1955.

Carter, Charles W. *A Contemporary Wesleyan Theology*. 2 vols. Grand Rapids: Francis Asbury, 1983.

Carradine, Beverly. *The Old Man*. Cincinnati: God's Revivalist, 1896.

Chafer, Lewis Sperry. *He That Is Spiritual*. 1918. Reprint, Philadelphia: Sunday School Times, 1924.

_____. *Systematic Theology*. 8 vols. Dallas: Dallas Seminary Press, 1948.

_____. *Grace*. Philadelphia: Sunday School Times, 1922.

Chrysostom, John. *Homilies on Romans*. *The Nicene and Post-Nicene Fathers*. Philip Schaff, ed. First Series. Vol. 11. 1889. Reprint, Grand Rapids: Eerdmans, 1979.

Clarke, Adam. *The Holy Bible, Containing the Old and New Testaments: The Text Carefully Printed from the Most Correct Copies of the Present Authorized Translations, Including the Marginal reading and Parallel Tests; with a Commentary and Critical Notes, Designed as a help to a Better Understanding of the Sacred Writings*. 6 vols. 1811-1825. Reprint, Nashville: Abingdon, 1950.

Clement of Alexandria. *Stromata*. *The Ante-Nicene Fathers*. Alexander Roberts and James Donaldson, eds. Vol. 2. 1905. Reprint, Grand Rapids: Eerdmans, 1979.

Clement of Rome. "Two Epistles Concerning Virginity." Alexander Roberts and James Donaldson, eds. 1903. Reprint, Grand Rapids: Eerdmans, 1978.

Coke, Thomas. *A Commentary on the Holy Bible.* 6 vols. London: G. Whitfield, 1801-1803.

Cox, Leo G. "Sin in Believers." *Wesleyan Theological Journal* 1:1 (Spring 1966) 27-32.

Cranfield, C. E. B. *International Critical Commentary: A Critical and Exegetical Commentary on the Epistle to the Romans.* 2 vols. Edinburgh: T&T Clark, 1975; 1979. [*ICC*]

Cyril of Jerusalem. *Catechetical* Lectures. Nicene *and Post-Nicene Fathers.* Philip Schaff and Henry Wace, eds. Second Series. Vol. 7. 1893. Reprint, Grand Rapids: Eerdmans, 1978.

Dana, H. E. and Julius R. Mantey. *A Manual Grammar of the Greek New Testament.* New York: Macmillan, 1955.

Dayton, Wilbur T. "Romans." *The Wesleyan Bible Commentary.* Charles W. Carter, ed. Vol. 5. Grand Rapids: Baker, 1966.

Dunn, James D. G. *Word Biblical Commentary: Romans 1-8.* Vol. 38A. Dallas: Word, 1988; *Romans 9-16.* Vol. 38B. Dallas: Word, 1988. [*WBC*]

Dunning, H. Ray. *Grace, Faith, and Holiness.* Kansas City: Beacon Hill, 1988.

Earle, Ralph. *Word Meanings in the New Testament.* 6 vols. Kansas City: Beacon Hill, 1974.

Fee, Gordon. *God's Empowering Presence: The Holy Spirit in the Letters of Paul.* Peabody, MA: Hendrickson, 1994.

Ferguson, Sinclair B. *The Holy Spirit.* Downers Grove, IL: InterVarsity, 1996.

Fletcher, John. *The Works of the Reverend John Fletcher.* 1833. Reprint, Salem, OH: Schmul, 1974.

Flew, R. Newton. *The Idea of Perfection in Christian Theology*. London: Oxford, 1934.

Fung, Ronald Y. K. "The Impotence of the Law: Toward a Fresh Understanding of Romans 7:14-25." *Scripture, Tradition, and Interpretation*. W. Ward Gasque and William Sanford LaSor, eds. Grand Rapids: Eerdmans, 1978.

Gagnon, Robert A. J. *The Bible and Homosexual Practice*. Nashville: Abingdon, 2001.

Gleason, Randall. "B. B. Warfield and Lewis S. Chafer on Sanctification." *Journal of the Evangelical Theological Society* 40:2 (June 1997) 241-256.

Graham, James. R. "Are There Carnal Christians?" Reprinted in A. J. Smith, *Bible Holiness and the Modern, Popular, Spurious*. Greensboro, NC: n. p. 1953. pp. 130-138. This book was reprinted by Fundamental Wesleyan Publishers as *Bible Holiness* in 1997. Graham's article is found on pp. 156-164.

Greathouse, William M. "Romans." *Beacon Bible Commentary*. Vol. 8. Kansas City: Beacon Hill, 1968.

_____ and George Lyons. *Romans 1-8. New Beacon Bible Commentary*. Kansas City: Beacon Hill, 2008.

_____. *From the Apostles to Wesley*. Kansas City: Beacon Hill, 1979.

Green, Joel B. and William H. Willimon, eds. *The Wesley Study Bible*. Nashville: Abingdon, 2009.

Gregory of Nyssa. *Against Eunomius. Nicene and Post-Nicene Fathers*. Philip Schaff and Henry Wace, eds. Second Series. Vol. 5. 1892. Reprint, Grand Rapids: Eerdmans, 1979.

Gregory of Nazianzen. *In Defense of His Flight to Pontus. Nicene and Post-Nicene Fathers*. Philip Schaff and Henry Wace, eds. Second Series. Vol. 7. 1893. Reprint, Grand Rapids: Eerdmans, 1978.

Grider, J. Kenneth. *Entire Sanctification: The Distinctive Doc-*

trine of Wesleyanism. Kansas City: Beacon Hill, 1980.

_____. *A Wesleyan-Holiness Theology.* Kansas City: Beacon Hill, 1994.

Godbey, W. B. *Commentary on the New Testament.* 7 vols. Cincinnati: Revivalist 1896-1900.

Harper, Albert F. ed. *The Wesley Bible.* Nashville: Thomas Nelson, 1990.

Haldane, Robert. *Exposition of the Epistle to the Romans.* 1847. Reprint, London: Banner of Truth, 1958.

Hendriksen, William. *New Testament Commentary: Romans.* Grand Rapids: Baker, 1981.

Hills, A. M. *Fundamental Christian Theology.* 1931. Reprint, two volumes in one. Salem, OH: Schmul, 1980.

Hodge, Charles. *Commentary on the Epistle to the Romans.* 1886. Reprint, Grand Rapids: Eerdmans, 1950.

Hoekema, Anthony A. "The Reformed View: Response to Walvoord." *Five Views on Sanctification.* Grand Rapids: Zondervan, 1987.

_____. "The Struggle Between the Old and New Natures in The Converted Man." *Bulletin of Evangelical Theological Society* 5 (March 1962) 42-50.

Howard, Richard E. *Newness of Life.* Kansas City: Beacon Hill, 1975.

Irenaeus. *Against Heresies. The Ante-Nicene Fathers.* Alexander Roberts and James Donaldson, eds. Vol. 1. 1885. Reprint, Grand Rapids: Eerdmans, 1979.

Jennings, Daniel R. "The Patristic Interpretation of Romans 7:14-25, Part 1. The Early Christian Witness to the Arminian Interpretation." *The Arminian Magazine* 27:2 (Fall 2009) 4-7; "Part 2. The Men Responsible for Introducing the Calvinistic Interpretation." 28:1 (Spring 2010) 3-5.

Jerome. *Letters. Nicene and Post-Nicene Fathers.* Philip Schaff and Henry Wace, eds. Second Series. Vol. 6. 1892. Reprint,

Grand Rapids: Eerdmans, 1979.

Johnson, Dennis E. "The Function of Romans 7:13-25 in Paul's Argument for the Law's Impotence and the Spirit's Power, and It's Bearing on the Schizophrenic 'I.'" *Resurrection and Eschatology: Theology in Service of the Church: Essays in Honor of Richard B. Gaffin, Jr.* Tipton, Lane G. and Jeffrey C. Waddington, eds. Phillipsburg, NJ: Presbyterian & Reformed, 2008.

Käsemann, Ernst. *Commentary on Romans*, G. W. Bromiley, transl. Grand Rapids: Eerdmans, 1980.

Keener Craig S. *The Mind of the Spirit: Paul's Approach to Transformed Thinking.* Grand Rapids: Baker, 2016.

Knox, John. *The Interpreter's Bible: Romans* [Exegesis]. Vol. 9. George Arthur Buttrick, ed. Nashville: Abingdon-Cokesbury, 1954.

Lactantius. *The Divine Institutes. The Ante-Nicene Fathers.* Alexander Roberts and James Donaldson, eds. Vol. 7. 1886. Reprint, Grand Rapids: Eerdmans, 1979.

Lake, Donald M. "Jacob Arminius' Contribution to a Theology of Grace." Clark H. Pinnock, ed. *Grace Unlimited.* Minneapolis: Bethany House, 1975.

Lange, John Peter. *A Commentary on the Holy Scriptures, Critical, Doctrinal, and Homiletical: With Special Reference to Ministers and Students.* Vol. 5. Transl. J. F. Hurst. Edited by Philip Schaff and M. B. Riddle. New York: Charles Scribner's Sons, 1899.

Lloyd-Jones, David Martyn. *The Law: Its Functions and Limits, An Exposition of Romans 7:1-8:4.* Grand Rapids: Zondervan, 1973.

Lucado, Max. *In the Grip of Grace.* Dallas: Word, 1996.

Luther, Martin. *Commentary on the Epistle to the Galatians.* Theodore Graebner, transl. 1535. Reprint, Grand Rapids, Michigan: Zondervan, 1949.

_____. *Dr. Martin Luther's House-Postil, or Sermons on the Gospels for the Sundays and Principle Festivals of the Church-Year*. 2nd ed. 2 vols. Columbus, OH: J. A. Schulze, 1884.

Macarius. *Fifty Spiritual Homilies of St. Macarius the Egyptian*. A. J. Mason, ed. London: SPK, 1921.

MacArthur, John F. Jr. *The MacArthur New Testament Commentary: Romans 1-8*. Chicago: Moody, 1991; *Romans 9-16*. Chicago: Moody, 1994.

_____. *The Gospel According to Jesus*. Grand Rapids: Zondervan, 1988.

Macknight, James. *A New Literal Translation from the Original Greek of all the Apostolical Fathers with a Commentary and Notes*. 1795. Reprint, Grand Rapids: Baker, 1984.

Marsh, Elmer G. *The Old Man*. Cincinnati: Revivalist, 1931.

McCant, Jerry. "The Wesleyan Interpretation of Romans 5-8." *Wesleyan Theological Journal* 16:1 (Spring, 1981) 68-84.

McCown, Wayne, ed. *The Reflecting God Study Bible*. Grand Rapids: Zondervan, 2000.

McLaughlin, George A. *Commentary on the Epistle of Paul to the Romans*. Chicago: Christian Witness, 1926.

McNeill, John T. ed. John Calvin, *Institutes of the Christian Religion*. 2 vols. ed. Philadelphia: Westminster, 1960.

McGonigle, Herbert Boyd. *Sufficient Saving Grace: John Wesley's Evangelical Arminianism*. Carlisle, Cumbria: Paternoster, 2001.

McPherson, Joseph D. "What Manner of Man Is He, Described in the Seventh of Romans? *The Arminian Magazine* 1:1 (Spring 1980) 6-8.

Methodius of Olympus. *The Discourse On the Resurrection*. *Ante-Nicene Fathers*. Alexander Roberts and James Donaldson, eds. Vol. 6. 1885. Reprint, Grand Rapids: Eerdmans, 1978.

Mickelsen, A. Berkeley. "Romans." *The Wycliffe Bible Commentary.* Everett F. Harrison, ed. Chicago: Moody, 1962.

Mitton, C. Leslie. "Romans vii. Reconsidered — I-III," *The Expository Times* 65:3-5 (Dec 1953 – Feb 1954) 78-81; 99-103; 132-135.

Moo, Douglas. *The Wycliffe Exegetical Commentary: Romans 1-8.* Kenneth Barker, ed. Chicago: Moody, 1991.

_____. *New International Commentary on the New Testament: The Epistle to the Romans.* Gordon Fee, ed. Grand Rapids: Eerdmans, 1996. [*NICNT*]

Morrison, H. C. *Baptism with the Holy Ghost.* 1900. Reprint, Salem, OH: Allegheny, 1978.

Murray, John. *The Epistle to the Romans: The New International Commentary on the New Testament.* 2 vols. Ned B. Stonehouse, ed. Grand Rapids: Eerdmans, 1959. [*NICNT*]

_____. *Principles of Conduct.* Grand Rapids: Eerdmans, 1957.

Needham, David C. *Birthright.* Portland: Multnomah, 1979.

Newell, William R. *Romans Verse by Verse.* Chicago: Moody Press, 1938.

Nichols, James and W. R. Bagnall, eds. The Writings of James Arminius. 3 vols. Grand Rapids: Baker Book House, 1956.

Oden, Thomas C. *Life in the Spirit: Volume Three of Systematic Theology.* San Francisco: HarperCollins, 1992.

Owen, John. *The Works of John Owen.* William H. Goold, ed. 16 vols. 1850-1853. Reprint, Edinburgh: Banner of Truth, 1967.

Packer, James I. *Keeping in Step with the Spirit.* Old Tappan, NJ: Revell, 1984.

_____. "The 'Wretched Man' Revisited." *Romans and the People of God: Essays in Honor of Gordon D. Fee on the Occasion of His 65th Birthday.* Sven K. Soderlund and N. T. Wright, eds. Grand Rapids: Eerdmans, 1999. 70-81.

Paulinus. *Letters of St. Paulinus of Nola*. Vol. 1. P. G. Walsh, transl. New York: Newman Press, 1966.

Peck, George. *The Scripture Doctrine of Christian Perfection*. 1842. Reprint, Salem, OH: Schmul, 1988.

Picirilli, Robert. *The Book of Romans*. Nashville: Randall House, 1975.

Pope, William Burt. *A Compendium of Christian Theology*. 3 vols. London: Wesleyan Conference Office, 1880.

_____. *The Prayers of St. Paul*. London: Charles H. Kelly, 1896.

Purkiser, W. T. *The Biblical Foundations*. Vol. 1 of *Exploring Christian Holiness*. Kansas City: Beacon Hill, 1983.

Ramm, Bernard. *Protestant Biblical Interpretation*. Grand Rapids: Baker, 1970.

Reymond, Robert. *A New Systematic Theology*. Nashville: Thomas Nelson, 1998.

Robertson, A. T. *Word Pictures in the New Testament*. 6 vols. Nashville: Broadman, 1931.

Rushdoony, Rousas J. *Romans & Galatians*. Vallecito, CA: Ross House, 1997.

_____. *Systematic Theology*. 2 vols. Vallecito, CA: Ross House, 1994.

Ryle, John Charles. *Holiness: Its Nature, Hindrances, Difficulties, and Roots*. 1877. Reprint, Welwyn: Evangelical Press, 1979.

Sanday, William and Arthur C. Headlam. *A Critical and Exegetical Commentary on the Epistle to the Romans: The International Critical Commentary*. 1895. Reprint, Edinburgh: T & T Clark, 1950. [*ICC*]

Schreiner, Thomas R. *Baker Exegetical Commentary on the New Testament: Romans*. Grand Rapids: Baker, 1998.

Scofield, C. I., ed. *The New Scofield Reference Bible*. New York: Oxford University Press, 1967.

_____. *Rightly Dividing the Word of Truth.* 1896. Reprint, Grand Rapids: Zondervan, 1972.

Shank, Robert. *Life in the Son.* Springfield, MO: Westcott, 1961.

Sproul, R. C. *The Gospel of God.* 1994. Reprint, Ross-shire, Scotland: Christian Focus, 1999.

_____, ed. *The Reformation Study Bible.* R. C. Sproul, ed. Nashville: Thomas Nelson, 2001. Formerly titled *The New Geneva Study Bible* (1995).

Stanglin, Keith D. and Thomas H. McCall. *Jacob Arminius: Theologian of Grace.* New York: Oxford, 2012.

Steele, Daniel. *Half-Hours with St. Paul.* 1894. Reprint, Rochester, PA: Schmul, 1959.

Steele, David N. and Curtis C. Thomas. *Romans: An Interpretive Outline.* Phillipsburg, NJ: Presbyterian and Reformed, 1963.

Stott, John R. W. *The Message of Romans: God's Good News for the World.* Downers Grove, IL: InterVarsity, 1994.

_____. *Men Made New: An Exposition of Romans 5-8.* 1966. Reprint, Grand Rapids: Baker, 1984.

Summers, Thomas O. *The Epistle of Paul, the Apostle, to the Romans, in the Authorized Version; with a New Translation and Commentary.* Nashville: Southern Methodist Publishing House, 1881.

Sutcliffe, Joseph. *A Commentary on the Old and New Testament.* 2 vols. 1834. Reprint, Salem, OH: Allegheny, 2000.

Taylor, Richard S. *Life in the Spirit.* Kansas City: Beacon Hill, 1966.

Terry, Milton S. *Biblical Hermeneutics.* 2nd ed. 1885. Reprint, Grand Rapids: Zondervan, 1974.

Tertullian. *On the Resurrection of the Flesh. The Ante-Nicene Fathers.* Alexander Roberts and James Donaldson, eds. Vol 3. 1885. Reprint, Grand Rapids: Eerdmans, 1978.

_____. *On Modesty. The Ante-Nicene Fathers.* Alexander

Roberts and James Donaldson, eds. Vol 4. 1885. Reprint, Grand Rapids: Eerdmans, 1979.

Tietz, Christiane. *Karl Barth: A Life in Conflict*. Transl, Victoria J. Barnett. Oxford, UK: Oxford University Press, 2021.

Walvoord, John. "The Augustinian-Dispensational Perspective." *Five Views on Sanctification*. Grand Rapids: Zondervan, 1987.

Wang, Joseph S. *Romans: Asbury Bible Commentary*. Eugene E. Carpenter and Wayne McCown, eds. Grand Rapids: Zondervan, 1992.

Warfield, Benjamin Breckinridge. *Perfectionism*. 2 vols. 1931. Reprint, Grand Rapids: Baker, 1981.

Watson, Richard. *Theological Institutes*. 2 vols. 1823-1829. Reprint, New York: Hunt & Eaton, 1889.

_____. *Conversations for the Young: Designed to Promote the Profitable Reading of the Holy Scriptures*. London: John Mason, 1830.

Wesley, John. *Explanatory Notes Upon the New Testament*. 1754. Reprint, Salem, OH: Schmul, 1976.

_____. *The Bicentennial Edition of the Works of John Wesley*. 35 vols. when complete. Frank Baker, ed. Nashville: Abingdon, 1975-. [*BE*]

Whedon, Daniel D. *Commentary on the New Testament*. 5 vols. 1860-1880. Reprint, Salem, OH: Schmul, 1977.

Wilder, Terry L. ed. *Perspectives On Our Struggle With Sin: Three Views of Romans 7*. Nashville: B&H, 2011.

Williams, Henry W. *An Exposition of St. Paul's Epistle to the Romans*. London: Wesleyan Conference Office, 1869.

Williams, William G. *An Exposition of the Epistle of Paul to the Romans*. New York: Eaton & Mains, 1902.

Witherington, Ben III. *The Problem with Evangelical Theology: Testing the Exegetical Foundations of Calvinism, Dispensationalism, and Wesleyanism*. Waco, TX: Baylor

University Press, 2006.
Wood, A. Skevington. *Life by the Spirit*. Grand Rapids: Zondervan, 1963. Also published as *Paul's Pentecost*. Exeter, Devon, England: Paternoster Press, 1963.
Wright, N. T. *The New Interpreter's Bible*. Vol. 10. Nashville: Abingdon, 2002. [*NIB*]
Wynkoop, Mildred. Foundations of Wesleyan-Arminian Theology. Kansas City: Beacon Hill Press, 1967.

www.ingramcontent.com/pod-product-compliance
Lightning Source LLC
Chambersburg PA
CBHW060202050426
42446CB00013B/2953